THE PACT

THE PACT

A UFC CHAMPION, A BOY WITH CANCER, AND
THEIR PROMISE TO WIN THE ULTIMATE BATTLE

CODY GARBRANDT

with **MARK DAGOSTINO**

WITHDRAWN

W Publishing Group

An Imprint of Thomas Nelson

Published in Nashville, Tennessee, by W Publishing, an imprint of Thomas Nelson.

Thomas Nelson titles may be purchased in bulk for educational, business, fund-raising, or sales promotional use. For information, please e-mail SpecialMarkets@ThomasNelson.com.

Any Internet addresses, phone numbers, or company or product information printed in this book are offered as a resource and are not intended in any way to be or to imply an endorsement by Thomas Nelson, nor does Thomas Nelson vouch for the existence, content, or services of these sites, phone numbers, companies, or products beyond the life of this book.

Library of Congress Control Number: 2018932138

ISBN 978-0-7852-1681-0 (HC)
ISBN 978-0-7852-1677-3 (eBook)

Printed in the United States of America

18 19 20 21 22 LSC 10 9 8 7 6 5 4 3 2 1

CONTENTS

CONTENTS

PREFACE

EXPECT THE UNEXPECTED

SOMETIMES YOU DON'T SEE THE FIGHT COMING.

Sometimes you get jumped from behind.

Sometimes you get sucker punched.

There's no way around it. It happens. To everyone.

The key, though? The key to surviving? The key to thriving? That all depends on what you do next. And what you do next? Well, that's up to you. Or, to be more accurate, that's between you and God.

What I've learned these last few years is that even when you think you're alone, fending for yourself against this world and everybody else in it, you're not. You're just not. When you watch for the signs, you realize God's actually got your back. He's put a whole army of allies around you who are ready to give you the strength you need to fight, to defend yourself, to rise up, to make it all the way to the top if that's where you want to go.

The thing is, those allies, those angels, those people who are here to lend you strength you didn't even know you had—they're not always who you'd expect them to be. And sometimes they come out of nowhere. They show up out of the blue and take you by surprise, just like the fight you didn't see coming. . . .

ONE

WANT TO KNOW WHAT I REMEMBER MOST ABOUT
my childhood?

Fighting.

Pick a time or a place in my hometown, and chances are I can tell you
about a fight that happened then or there—one that I watched, or one that I
got into.

Fighting's how I marked my time.

Like in fifth grade, I remember fighting this kid Jimmy outside his house
over by the football stadium. I was kicking the spit out of him when a guy
drove up in an unmarked sedan. He was a real responsible-looking dude, a
grown-up authority-figure type for sure, but he didn't get out or try to stop the
fight or anything. Instead, this guy pulled up and looked right at me and said,
"Well, I can tell you're gonna be seeing a lot of me."

I looked back at him and yelled, "Get lost, man! This is none of your
business!"

When he left, I turned to one of the other kids who was standing around
watching us fight and said, "Who was that?"

"Oh, that's Jimmy's probation officer."

That's right. A fifth-grader had a probation officer. He wasn't the only
one, either. And here's the really crazy part: Jimmy's probation officer drove
up right in the middle of me whaling on him and didn't do anything to stop
it—because fighting was that much a part of life where we lived.

There's a saying around these parts: "If you're looking for help, call 911. If you're looking for trouble, call 922."

"The 922." That's the nickname for the little corner of Ohio I called home. It comes from our telephone exchange. Not the area code—that would be too big and nonspecific—but the next three digits after that.

My hometown of Uhrichsville, Ohio, is a Midwestern town full of old brick buildings and empty storefronts. Back in the late 1800s, it was a booming place—a town that billed itself as the "clay capital of the world." A major east-west railroad line runs right through the middle of it, and all sorts of businesses grew up around those tracks. It was probably someplace really great to live before all the jobs washed out for reasons no one seems to remember. Before so many people were left struggling just to pay their bills. Long before I was born.

Uhrichsville and its neighboring twin town of Dennison make up one combined small-town community here, and over at the Dennison Railroad Depot Museum, the streetlights are decorated with red, white, and blue banners that say "Dreamsville, USA." That was the nickname the town took on during World War II—which seems pretty funny to me, because nowadays the only thing most people in our corner of Ohio ever dream about is finding a way out.

My family, the Garbrandts, were pretty well known in the twin cities way before I came along. I guess you could say we had a reputation.

Growing up, we weren't the sort of family that went skiing together or hiking together or swimming together. I didn't even know any families that did that kind of stuff. Instead, we were a family that went to fights together: wrestling matches, boxing matches, neighborhood fights, bar brawls, it didn't matter. We went to fights and witnessed fights and talked about fights and fighters almost as much as we got into fistfights and fought with each other over every little thing every chance we got.

Maybe if I'd been born to a family of doctors or scientists or something I'd have spent my childhood hitting the books. Instead, I spent my childhood just plain hitting and getting hit and hitting back whenever I could.

Some of my earliest memories in life are of getting into it with my older brother, Zach. He's only ten months older than me, but he was always a whole lot bigger than me and naturally stronger than me, and it seemed like anything I did could set him off. I'd grab a toy that was his or say something he didn't like or look at him the wrong way, and he'd start whaling on me. I'm talking really young, like when we were three, four, five years old.

In some other family, I suppose the dad would've been there to step in and stop all that fighting. But our dad was in prison for most of our childhood. He's still in prison as I write this book. My mom tried to step in, but she just couldn't seem to stop us.

Occasionally Zach would beat me up pretty bad—so I learned to fight back pretty quick.

I think the first time I really hurt Zach (not that he would admit this) was when I was still a preschooler. We were playing Three Musketeers out in the woods somewhere, and we got into a fight. I cracked Zach in the head with a stick—cut his head right open. Mom wasn't too happy about that, but after all the beatings he'd given me, she told him it served him right.

I got into my first street fight in preschool too. Our mother put us in the Moravian day-care center, a local Christian-based school, while she went to work. My poor mom. She got the call that day because some kid bit my finger and I hauled off and socked him in the mouth.

It was just the beginning.

I was six years old when I got my first concussion. Zach and I were playing some sort of a no-rules hockey game on rollerblades in my grandparents' basement across town. Everything we did turned into a fight, so this was no different. I tried to get away from him and ran up the stairs with my rollerblades on, but Zach threw a basketball and knocked my legs out from under me. I fell all the way down the stairs and bashed my head on the cement floor. My first knockout.

I remember being so scared when I woke up in the hospital not knowing where I was or what had happened. We left there with a big old X-ray of my head, though, and I brought it into school for show-and-tell. I thought it was cool!

That's the thing: It was cool. I loved to fight. I didn't mind getting hurt. I liked to try new moves that might take Zach down, to push myself and learn to hit harder than he did. Those fights, as crazy as they got sometimes, were fun to me. And to Zach.

What Zach did to me on the stairs wasn't cool, though, and even at that young age I was patient enough to wait and exact my revenge when the time was right—right when he would least expect it.

Zach and I weren't allowed to play in the basement at my grandparents' house for about a month after I got that concussion, but finally one day after school Grandma said we could play. We were sitting on the cold cement floor putting on our rollerblades, and Zack kept looking at me like, "This is gonna be fun! We get to play!" He was all excited, and so was I—but for a very different reason.

I thought, *I remember when you kicked me down those steps.* So I laced up my rollerblades real quick, and while he was still busy tying his second skate, I lifted my leg up as high as I could and kicked him right on the side of his head—not with the toe of the skate, but with the big block brake on the back of the skate. In an instant, Zach's temple swelled up like an egg. And then it kept growing. It ballooned out a good two or three inches from the side of his face before Grandma got some ice on it.

Our mom couldn't take us anywhere without us fighting. She couldn't even take us to the mall without Zach and me getting into it and wrestling under the clothing racks. So she decided to channel that energy of ours into something a little more purposeful. And the only thing she could think of was to throw us into the most popular sport in our town: wrestling.

It seems like everyone in the 922 is into wrestling, the way people in other towns might be into their *Friday Night Lights*–style football games. The state wrestling championships held by Claymont High School are all listed on a sign off one of the highway exits into town. There are plaques with the names and photos of the top wrestlers hung on the walls in our schools. Our local newspaper, the *Times–Reporter*, dedicates all kinds of ink to the local and state wrestling scene. Wrestlers were pretty much the closest thing we had to stars and heroes in our twin cities when I was growing up, and I remember getting excited about going to matches when I was as young as five years old.

As soon as my mom saw that Zach and I were into the sport, she pushed us to be good at it. No sooner did she get us into the school programs than she got us into after-school wrestling camps, too, where she took all of the coaches' advice on how to turn us into great wrestlers. In grammar school she had us disciplined, man. She made sure we were on time for practices, and she made sure we started eating right, even though she wasn't a healthy eater herself. She went out and bought some cookbooks and started cooking veggies, and getting us some lean protein through chicken breasts cooked on a George Foreman Grill so the fat all drained away.

Mom always made sure our homework was done, too, because we couldn't be on a wrestling team if we didn't keep our grades up. We'd get home from school, and she would bring us a snack, then take us straight to wrestling. We'd come home from wrestling, and she'd make us shower to get the stink off us. Then we'd eat dinner, finish up any homework, and go to bed.

When the school week was over, she'd take us around to wrestling tournaments, entering us in matches against kids from other towns on Fridays and Saturdays. Sometimes it was a two-hour drive in each direction, but she never let up. She engraved us with the grind.

Starting in first grade, I proved myself to have some unique talents on the wrestling mat. We had novice tournaments in grade school. We would do a week of wrestling, then go to a two-hour session taught by the high school kids on Saturday. Then the tournament itself would be held at the high school— and I'd win every single year.

My mom said I was her "little monkey" because that's what I looked like out on the mat, scrambling all over the place and scoring in ways my opponents couldn't seem to keep up with. I would roll across the mat and run from one side to the other to keep my opponents and everyone else thinking, *What is he doing?* I just had fun with it.

Zach and I both loved the adrenaline rush of seeing an opponent right there in front of us and then figuring out how to take him down. We went to each match believing that we'd trained harder than anyone else and knowing we only had one shot to prove what all that training had done.

In some ways Zach pushed me even harder than my mom did. I remember going to wrestling practice at nine or ten years old and thinking the coach was a real jerk for pushing kids so hard they would cry. I can remember the first time a coach tried to get us to do a hundred push-ups. I was probably only fifty push-ups in when my arms started shaking and I started to feel the burn in my forearms. By sixty I was ready to collapse. But the coach kept yelling, "If your knees touch the ground, you've gotta start all over at zero!"

It seemed like all of the other kids were dropping to the mat all around us. But I looked over at Zach—he was pushing himself harder and harder. He looked back at me and said, "Don't touch your knee! We're not squealing out!" And I kept going just to show him that I could.

I also kept going for my mom. I wasn't sure what kinds of families the other kids came from or why they were willing to let themselves cry and give up during practice, but I knew my mom was sacrificing big-time to get us into those elite-level wrestling camps at a young age. She sacrificed a lot. She went most of those years without buying herself even one new pair of shoes, just so she could afford those camps. I would picture those worn-out old shoes of hers and think, *There is no way I'm gonna cry and drop out just 'cause it hurts a little!*

She sacrificed for us so we could do what we loved to do. And what we loved to do was wrestle. To us it was worth all the training, all the intense discipline that only grew more intense as we got older.

It wasn't just my mom and our coaches that pushed Zach and me into the discipline of wrestling, though. We had a couple of other important influences—one of them good and one of them not so good.

The not-so-good influence was my dad, and part of the reason I dedicated myself to wrestling was because I didn't want to wind up living the life he'd lived. My mom was still just a teenager when we were both born. She's the one who held down a job, went to school, graduated, and took care of us while our dad was in and out of prison for theft and assault and drug charges.

My dad's father, our grandfather, had gone to prison too. And from what we heard, whenever he came out he used to beat my dad and his brothers pretty bad when they were kids. I guess the cycle of that kind of violence looks pretty obvious from the outside, but it just seemed normal to us. Our grandfather mellowed out in his old age, so Zach and I never knew him as a violent guy. But his influence rubbed off on more than just my dad. My uncles wound up going to prison too. My dad and his brothers were all tatted-up tough guys who kept finding trouble wherever they went in their teens and early twenties—and those were basically the only male role models we had as kids.

I got pretty tired of the small-town mentality where so many of my peers and even some of my teachers kept telling me, "You're gonna turn out just like your father."

Maybe part of the reason they thought that of me is because I struggled in school. I had a hard time keeping my head in my books because I loved to fight, and I might have loved it just a little bit more than most of my peers. Maybe that's why my dad and uncles got into trouble too. Maybe that's why they ended up in jail. Maybe it's genetic.

All the grown-ups around me kept telling me that if I kept on fighting, I wouldn't amount to anything. They were looking out for me, but I wanted to fight. I was driven to fight. Even as I got into middle school and it started to become clear that I was a good wrestler, there were still people telling me that I wouldn't get anywhere. If I kept fighting, they said—even when "fighting" meant wrestling—the only place I'd wind up is in prison next to my dad.

I didn't want that. But sometimes it just seemed like it was in the cards. No matter how much discipline my mom imposed, fighting was in my blood, and fighting was just what kids did in the 922. I couldn't help myself.

Like in fifth grade, when I got into that fight with Jimmy and found out that he had a parole officer—I don't even remember what that fight was about. Maybe a girl. Who knows? When you're fighting in fifth and sixth grade, those fights are pretty pointless.

The thing that some people don't get about the way we fought, though, was that we could go right back to being normal afterward. Zach and I never hated each other. We'd both wipe off the dirt and blood and sit down and have dinner together. I'm sure me and this kid Jimmy saw each other at school the next day and just nodded hello in the hall or something. Zach and I played football as kids, too, and we could get into huge fights with our teammates but still work well together on the field. It was all just part of life.

I was rarely the person who started a fight, but I was happy to take on the fights that came to me. Going all the way back to first grade, there were times when fights broke out spontaneously. There were also times when someone would call a kid out for something and agree to meet at some specific location to fight after school. Everyone would hear about it and circle up to check it out, and sometimes kids in the crowd would start fighting each other while they watched. It seemed like there was never an adult around to stop it. Maybe because all of the adults in the 922 had grown up fighting too.

I learned as I got older that the culture didn't change after school was finished. There were bar fights and street brawls happening almost every night of the week. There were spots, including the pump house on the outskirts of town, where people would show up to fight after they were called out, and crowds would gather to watch and fight themselves. It's just how people in our corner of the country proved their worth and found their place in the world. I don't know why. It's just how it was—and still is.

I mentioned there was another influence in my life, though—a good influence. A person who would try to teach us that fighting could have a point. Who taught Zach and me that fighting could make a positive difference in our lives.

This man believed in fighting.

He preached to us about fighting in the same way he talked to us about God.

He believed in us, and he made us believe that learning to be great fighters would be good for us no matter what. "You have to fight for what you want in life," he told us. "Sometimes you have to fight just to survive."

TWO

I HONESTLY CAN'T IMAGINE HOW MY LIFE WOULD have turned out if my Uncle Bob hadn't stepped in when he did. It's almost like God sent him back into the ring just to save Zach and me.

Just like my dad and his other brother, Mike, my Uncle Bob wound up in prison on felony charges before he finished high school. But unlike Mike, who spent a good portion of his life in prison, or my dad, who was in and out on worse and worse charges the older he got, Uncle Bob went to prison just once, on a twenty-three-month stint, and came out a changed man.

First, he studied behind bars and graduated high school. Or, as he puts it in his own unique way of talking, "I didn't go to school, but I learned my schooling in prison."

Second, Uncle Bob found God in prison.

It happened when he woke up in his cell one night unable to breathe. He told us he felt like he was being smothered. The weight on his chest was unbearable. He couldn't get any oxygen into his lungs no matter how hard he tried. Something invisible was pinning him down to that prison bed, and he thought for sure he was going to die.

In a state of panic, unable to move or to call for help, he did something he'd never done before. He closed his eyes, and he prayed.

Help me, God! God, please help me! he cried out in his mind.

That's when the presence moved off him, and a tremendous weight lifted from his chest. He could suddenly breathe, and in one great gasp he inhaled the purest, most beautiful air he'd ever tasted.

He asked one of his fellow inmates about the experience. An inmate he trusted. An inmate who was known to pray. And that inmate told him there was no doubt: he had been saved. God had answered his prayer and removed a demon from Uncle Bob's body.

From that moment forward, Uncle Bob was a believer. More than that, he was a changed man. He started reading the Bible. He prayed every day. He made up his mind to stop drinking and to stop doing drugs. And although he was still a young man who easily could have gone back to his partying ways once he got out of prison, he didn't.

As the cold metal doors slammed closed behind him, Uncle Bob knew he would never hear that sound again. And he decided to do what he could to end the vicious family cycle that had led him to prison in the first place. He would show up and act as a stand-in father figure for his brother's kids—namely, Zach and me.

He showed up in the nick of time—just as we were starting to really hurt each other in our basement and backyard brawls. And he did everything he could to help my mom channel our energy into fighting of a different sort.

Before he went to prison, Uncle Bob had showed some real promise as a boxer. There was no place he liked to be any better than in a gym somewhere, hitting the heavy bag, sparring in the ring, prepping for a future he believed he could conquer. He set his sights on the Olympics, and he even had a coach who was ready to take him all the way.

Instead, he got sucked into the underbelly of the 922 and wound up in prison.

Once he was out, though, Uncle Bob went right back to that dream of his, and he decided to bring me and Zach along for the ride—not only to watch him as he trained for the next Olympic trials, but also to serve as our personal coach and to train us to be great fighters ourselves.

There was just one thing standing in his way: our mom. She hated boxing. She refused to see her kids get their heads bashed in, and she insisted that Uncle Bob train us in wrestling instead. But he didn't. He left that to the school and camp coaches, and whenever my mother wasn't around, he secretly trained us to box.

I'll never forget how amazing it was to watch Uncle Bob work out in the gym. He was focused. He was fierce. He would work hard and get all sweaty and have this look in his eyes like he could rip any opponent to shreds. And then he'd stop and give us his full attention, showing us how to stand so we were balanced and less likely to get knocked over, how to hold our fists, how to punch with the power of our whole bodies behind us so we would inflict the most damage on our opponents and not hurt ourselves while we did it.

Since our hands were small, he'd put his flip-flops on his hands and have us punch them like they were training paddles. Once we knew what we were doing, he'd put gloves on the both of us and have us spar in front of all of the other boxers. He'd take us into the backyard of my grandparents' house and set up sparring matches with other kids from around town, too, dressing us up in big gloves and pads and headgear and laughing like crazy as we went at it.

He would drive us around to watch wrestling tournaments and boxing matches, sometimes scaring us half to death as he flew down the highway at 120 miles per hour in his big old truck. And then, on Sundays, he'd take us to church.

I hadn't been to church a whole lot before Uncle Bob stepped in. My mother always believed in a higher power but was never a religious woman. And my grandparents took us a few times to this over-the-top, cultlike church where people around us all started talking in "tongues." I just didn't feel comfortable there at all, so I tried to avoid it as best I could. (Zach and I were both baptized in that church, though, because my grandfather offered to pay us fifty dollars if we did it. So we did it!)

Going to church with Uncle Bob was different, though. He'd talk about God and how God had changed his life and how important it was for us to have the Lord Jesus in our lives too. It was impossible not to get excited when he shared that part of himself, because he talked about God and Jesus with as much passion as he talked about boxing. I didn't follow everything he tried to tell us at first, and I didn't have any understanding of who Jesus was, but this nondenominational church he took us to in town was full of really nice people.

The minister always had something interesting to say, too, and I remember thinking a lot of times that whatever he spoke about on Sundays seemed to connect with whatever I was going through that week. Maybe I'd gotten in some trouble and needed to ask for forgiveness. Or maybe I'd walked past someone who seemed sad or hurt and I ought to think next time about turning around and helping that person out. Or maybe I was struggling and doing the wrong thing when I knew I ought to be doing the right thing. His words just seemed to hit home with me all the time. I can't explain it. There was something peaceful and comforting about being in that place.

I think Zach and I would have followed Uncle Bob anywhere—and we did. We followed him into bars more than once, even though we weren't even ten years old. We followed him up onto rooftops and into big holes in the dirt before the concrete was poured on construction sites. He didn't think twice about us possibly getting hurt, so neither did we.

We didn't think of him as a father figure—more as a friend. And yet we couldn't have asked for a better father figure, even if we'd known what we needed. He was constantly in our ears, saying, "Don't do drugs. Drugs are always a losing game." Or, "Don't be like your dad or your uncle. Don't be like I was when I was a kid." He wanted us to make something of ourselves and to "stay away from gangs."

That last part always made us laugh. There were no gangs to speak of in rural Ohio. But we knew what he meant. He wanted us to stay out of trouble and not run with the wrong people. "All that'll get you is thrown in jail," he reminded us again and again.

He kept on us about staying in school too—doing our homework and not skipping out. He was always telling us how important our education was.

But the one thing Uncle Bob kept hammering into our heads more than anything else, over and over, was the idea that fighting could be our ticket to everything we wanted. He truly believed that. "You want to make it out of here? You want to be a millionaire?" he said. "Fight."

God and boxing were Uncle Bob's saviors. He thought they could save us too.

Becoming a millionaire boxing champ wasn't in the cards for Uncle Bob himself. He hadn't had the family support he needed as a teenager, and going to prison meant he'd missed the Olympic trials he'd been training for. And once he was out of prison and on a better path, ready to tackle his dream, the dream kept dodging him.

He actually made it to a qualifying fight for the Olympic trials in his twenties, only to get robbed in a bout everyone seemed to agree was called unfairly. Even then he qualified as an alternate to the Olympics, but he never got a chance to go for the gold.

By that time he'd gotten married and had a kid of his own. His wife didn't want him to keep boxing for another four years to take another shot, and his prospects of making any money from boxing on the local circuit were slim. Plus, his priorities had shifted away from that life. So he started his own concrete business and threw his heart and soul into it.

Uncle Bob grew his little company into a big success, and he never stopped taking care of Zach and me while he did it. He was that one uncle who always stopped by and took us out to dinner or to buy us something we needed. He even took us to Sea World one time.

And he never, ever stopped training us.

I forget exactly how old Zach and I were when we saw the film *Vision Quest* for the first time. People who grew up in the eighties probably remember that movie because it featured some Madonna music and starred Matthew Modine. But for anyone interested in wrestling, it's a hugely motivating film.

We were way too young to see it according to most people's standards. I think it's rated R—for audiences seventeen and older—and we definitely weren't that old. But we started a lot of things young. Watching this wrestler get down on himself, cheat and eat pizza, then get inspired and make love to his girl before his big match—that stuff sticks with you. I don't know how many times I've watched and rewatched that movie, or at least parts of it, since then. Every wrestling season for sure. I grew up on it.

Maybe that movie is part of the reason why I started having my own visions and imagining my own quest for greatness when I was really young.

I didn't really understand the power of visualization back then. I didn't read any motivational books until I was older. But by the time I was eight or nine years old, I found myself visualizing all the time.

For example, I vividly remember going to sleep at night and visualizing myself riding a dirt bike. I knew it was something we could never afford, and my mom had said there was no way we'd ever get one. But I'd wake up crying sometimes because I wanted that bike so bad. I would see it in my dreams. I could feel myself riding it. I could hear the buzz of the engine and feel the bumps on the dirt trail and the wind rushing through my helmet. I'd wake up and cry when I realized that vision wasn't real.

But then one Christmas morning I woke up and there it was: a rusty old dirt bike under the Christmas tree. My vision came true! I swear I made it real just by imagining it hard enough.

That's powerful, I thought.

That happened right around the same time my mother remarried for the second time. Our new stepdad, Tim, was a hardworking guy, and he wanted to step up and do the right thing by my mother in such a big way that he actually adopted Zach and me.

I think I was in fourth grade when Tim took Zach and me to the state wrestling tournaments for the first time. They were held at the Jerome Schottenstein Center in Columbus, so everyone called them the Schottensteins. Wrestling was humongous in Ohio, and the winners of the state tournament were just bad dudes. Everyone respected those guys, whoever they were.

We had nosebleed seats in this arena full of thousands of people, and we could barely see the wrestlers on the mats below. They looked like ants. We had to use binoculars. But I didn't care. I thought being there was the greatest thing in the world. I left there with visions of wrestling on those mats in front of that crowd and winning that state championship myself. I went home with the announcer's voice echoing in my head, and I swear I could hear him calling out my name. I would sit in class in school and doodle about being the champion. I would fall asleep envisioning my winning moment, hearing the roar of the crowd, and then dream about it all while I slept.

After that first trip to the Schottensteins, my brother and I started to live and breathe wrestling. All we wanted to do was train.

I think any high school wrestler can tell you about the focus and effort it takes to cut weight, watch what you eat, train on top of that, and then compete, get ready for the next match, and cut weight again. Zach and I were doing that in grammar school. There were times when we would cut weight by fasting and doing all sorts of hard-core aerobic exercises, sweating out water weight, even taking diuretics when we were a little older to drop every ounce we could just to wrestle in a school match on a Wednesday. Then, once we'd made weight, we'd splurge and eat like crazy after it was over—only to spend the next three days cutting multiple pounds again so we could wrestle the Friday, Saturday, and Sunday tournaments.

For Christmas and birthdays, Zach and I no longer asked for bikes or toys. We wanted gear. On one Christmas morning we got weight sets. On another, we got new wrestling shoes. My mom had to force me to take those new wrestling shoes off in bed because I wanted to sleep in them, I loved them so much. I still remember the sound of her tearing the Velcro open and pulling them off of my feet when I was half asleep.

I loved every one of those presents. I was so thankful for them.

As we headed into middle school, my mom and Tim and Uncle Bob all decided we deserved to start training with the best of the best, and we found the best at a gym in Urbana, Ohio—a two-and-a-half-hour drive from Uhrichsville. My adoptive father used to drive us all that way to practices two days a week after school. We'd do our homework down there, train, then come all the way back. He'd get us something to eat from Subway or something. And then he'd have to drive an hour in the other direction to get to work.

That was some serious dedication right there.

Then my mom or Uncle Bob would drive us the forty-five minutes to the Schottenstein Center for open wrestling tournaments on the weekends. Wrestling on those mats in that big arena wasn't some far-off dream. I found out I could get into those tournaments right away, and because I worked so hard and was so dedicated to training, I started winning right away too. That vision I had of myself wrestling for a state championship in those open matches became real in no time.

It wasn't long before we discovered there were open tournaments all over the place. So we convinced our little family support troop to start taking us to open matches in West Virginia and Pennsylvania—which meant that my brother and I would sometimes wrestle Friday, Saturday, and Sunday every week. We got something like a hundred or two hundred matches per year under our belts as kids. And like anything else in life, the more we did it—the more we focused on it and the harder we worked at it—the better we got.

It didn't take long for us to discover that we could enter national open tournaments as well. Zach and I both made it onto "Team Ohio," which is made up of the best kids in the state. So we wound up being team players, wrestling in Iowa against California kids and New Jersey kids. It was cool. We'd see these big top studs coming in on a team from Montana or somewhere, and Zach and I would look at each other thinking the exact same thing: *Whoa. Those guys are gonna get beat up!*

We were fearless because we were good. My uncle kept training us to box, in secret, and there was something about that combination of training in two sports at once that gave us an edge—learning how to be light and quick on our feet at the same time we learned about using our whole bodies on the mat. We were unstoppable.

Not that it was a straight line to greatness. It wasn't. We won more than we lost, right from the start. But we did lose now and then—partly because we were chasing greatness while life kept throwing up roadblocks. For one, we sometimes found ourselves wrestling with injuries sustained in one of our after-school street fights. Zach grew tall and muscular by the time he was in eighth grade, so not many kids wanted to get into fights with him. They could see they were outmatched. But I stayed small. I didn't look like much of a threat. And I think more kids than ever wanted to get into fights with me just because they knew I was a good wrestler. They wanted to knock me down just to prove I wasn't all that, or to prove they were better than me.

They never did, though. Sometimes things got broken up before they ended, but I never lost a street fight. Ever.

Even with all of the distractions, I managed to stay focused on wrestling most of the time, and that was enough to get me where I wanted to go. My visions quickly shifted from winning a Schottenstein to winning a national tournament. I focused on it the same way I did the state tournaments: I could hear the announcer in my ear, see myself pinning my opponent in front of a stadium full of people, and hear the roar of the crowd. It was real to me. I just had to get there.

I was never the biggest or the strongest guy, even within my weight class. So I learned to work with what I had. And what I had, thanks in large part to my Uncle Bob's training, was speed and precision. At one tournament I looked at my opponent and figured out how I could take him down before the match even started. I just saw it. I knew what to do. So when the whistle blew, I pulled a 360 double leg and cradled the kid. The match was over in fifteen seconds.

My brother was standing on the sidelines and was blown away. He yelled, "Holy sh-t!" The coach and some parents reprimanded him for the language, but they had a look on their faces that said "holy sh-t" too!

One time during a state tournament, I was down in the semifinals. I'd gotten beat the year before, and I just refused to let that happen again. So even though this kid almost had me, with one leg wrapped in so I couldn't catch my balance and I was hopping, I decided to do something no one ever would expect. I did a back flip. I flipped myself right over the kid, and no sooner did I land one foot on the ground than I took him down and scored a point.

After pulling something like that, going on to win the tournament was pretty easy. Every other kid in the building was scared I might do something they'd never seen before, and that gave me all the edge I needed.

On Sundays, when Uncle Bob took us to church, I would thank God for giving me the abilities I had. At night I would pray to God to help make my vision come true—to help me win a national title.

I also made a deal with my mom—about tattoos.

I looked up to a lot of wrestlers at Claymont High School, not to mention in the professional wrestling world, and a lot of the best wrestlers had tattoos. My dad had tattoos. My Uncle Bob had tattoos. I didn't want to wait until I was older to get a tattoo myself, so Zach and I both made a deal with my mom that if we won at states and qualified for nationals that year, she would let us both get a tattoo.

I was so excited about it that in my free time I'd go to the library, look up all sorts of tattoo art, and print out design ideas. I wanted something cool. I wanted something meaningful.

Toward the end of my eighth-grade year, Zach and I managed to do better than just qualify for nationals. We both won national titles. And my mom made good on her promise: she took Zach and me to a tattoo parlor and signed off on our ink.

I knew what I wanted, but I made Zach go first. He wound up getting a big cross on his thigh with the words, "Only God Can Judge Me."

I decided to get inked with a cross too. After all the tattoo ideas I'd looked at, including all sorts of skulls and other tough-guy ink that you'd expect a fighter to wear on his body, I chose the cross because it grounded me. I wanted my first tattoo to be something meaningful, and my faith in God was about as meaningful as anything I could think of.

I put that design of a cross with a ribbon on it on my back because through all the ups and downs I'd experienced in my life, between my dad's absence and my mom's rocky relationships and our struggles with money and everything else, I knew God had my back. Whether I went to church on Sunday mornings with Uncle Bob or whether we skipped a few weeks, it didn't matter. It wasn't about church. It wasn't about religion. It was about knowing there was something—Somebody—more than just me. He was listening. I knew it. I felt it, the same way I knew what it felt like to win a big wrestling title before I ever stepped foot onto the mat.

No matter what happened next, that symbol of my personal faith was now etched on my back and would follow me everywhere I went. I could never forget about it. It was permanent.

THREE

I HAD ONE GOAL AS A FRESHMAN IN HIGH SCHOOL: I wanted to win the state wrestling championship. No one from Claymont High School had ever won that title as a freshman, and I wanted to be the first.

Having already won a series of open tournaments and even a national title, I was pretty sure I could do it. In fact, I was pretty sure I could conquer the world—and I wasn't the only one. Our high school wrestling coach, Coach Eric Toukonen, had been keeping an eye on me since I was in middle school. He kept telling me he was absolutely positive I could be the first kid in the history of Ohio high school wrestling to win the state championship all four years.

Coach Toukonen was like our own version of the "Bud Kilmer" character from *Varsity Blues.* He was the coach everyone knew and loved, with his slicked-back hair and seemingly endless dedication to the sport. Everyone in town looked up to the guy and respected what he'd done to put Claymont High wrestling on the map.

It does something to you when someone who's that influential in your hometown tells you something so hopeful. It fills you with confidence. It might even make you a little cocky—and I was. But cocky seemed to work for me. The other wrestlers seemed to watch me and want to learn from me, and maybe they even looked up to me a little as we pushed ourselves in the weight room. That felt good. I loved showing them some of the stuff I'd learned from wrestling camps, along with some of the striking techniques my Uncle Bob had been secretly teaching me in the boxing ring.

Coach was like another father figure to me. He was almost like a god in some ways, we all just looked up to him so much. I can still remember what it felt like every time he walked that stocky frame of his through the big brown door to the gymnasium. The whole room just came alive.

He was strict with us. He was hard on us. He wanted us to be the best, and we were. Claymont High School had a long reputation for winning tournaments against much bigger schools. Schools with much more funding. Schools that recruited wrestlers from other districts even. But we were this low-income, hard-grinding school that just produced great wrestlers year after year. And so much of that was due to Coach himself.

Coach and I would wrestle full-on sometimes. He was significantly older and bigger and stronger, but he wouldn't go easy on me. He'd push me. He wanted me to know that if I could go toe-to-toe with him, I could easily dominate other kids in my own weight class.

In many ways, Coach and I developed a friendship. My relationship with him felt supportive, almost like my relationship with Uncle Bob felt supportive.

Coach always played old-school classic rock on a boom box to keep us motivated. I'd never paid any attention to that kind of music until Coach Toukonen put it on. Led Zeppelin, Van Halen, Queen—any band with lots of fast-driving, hard-pounding drums and guitars—just seemed to get the blood pumping. He played AC/DC's *Back in Black* CD so much I must've memorized the entire thing before the season was out.

Using music and movies to visualize the battles and successes that lay ahead was a huge part of my routine. I knew the voice of the announcer at those state tournaments, and I could hear that voice in my head announcing the winner: "112-pound state champion, a freshman, from Uhrichsville, Claymont—Cody Garbrandt!"

I would doodle "State Champion Cody Garbrandt" everywhere—on my planner, in my books. Some people would tease me about it, like, "Yeah, man. You keep dreaming." But I believed it, and I just kept writing it down over and over and over again. I was so focused on grinding that year that my grades slipped a bit. I struggled with school. I couldn't help it. My mom would make me sit at the kitchen table for hours sometimes, making sure all of my work got done. But schoolwork just wasn't my thing.

Wrestling was my thing.

I wrestled a solid forty matches that season and won almost all of them. Still, my weight class was the most crowded in the state, and it was filled with talented competitors from other schools. So when it came time for states, even with my strong record, I was projected to take ninth place.

I liked that.

I'd seen the Rocky movies. I'd watched *Rudy*. I liked coming in as the underdog—the dark horse who could surprise a lot of people. The fighter nobody saw coming.

I guess I've had a natural affection for the underdog my whole life, including the underdogs at my school.

For example, I hated how a lot of kids would make fun of the challenged or mentally handicapped kids who came out for sports. They saw them as a distraction or a drawback or a waste of time for the team. And I was always like, "It's amazing that these guys want to wrestle!" I was always cool with them and helped them out or went out of my way to get them motivated.

I remember one kid, Billy, who had some challenges other kids didn't. But man, he had the biggest heart. He loved playing football and loved wrestling. He'd come to practice every day and run through our drills with us. Other kids would be complaining, and he'd just have the biggest smile on his face. He might have been less fortunate, but he was so happy to be there working out with us that I just thought it was the coolest thing ever. Why would anyone want to pick on a kid like that?

To me it's an inspiration to watch an underdog go for it. They deserve to be applauded, not put down, for the extra effort they put in. I remember sometimes no one wanted to sit with Billy on the bus rides to tournaments. But I did. I sat with him all the time.

There was another kid named Isaac who was in my homeroom from seventh grade all the way through senior year, and it seemed like everyone picked on him. He was super smart, but maybe a little socially awkward. So what? When we saw each other in the hallways, he'd always say, "What's up, Cody?"

and give me a rock pound. I'd see him running on the west side of town, running to the library to get books, and he'd rock-pound my fist on the street when he ran by too. We were buds. In high school he took his love of running and tried out for the track team. All that back and forth to the library had been good training. He was good! He was a happy-go-lucky kid who didn't deserve to be picked on at all.

It was just a couple of weeks before the sectional tournament, a must-do event on the road to the state championships, when some kid tripped Isaac in the cafeteria. It happened right in front of me. Isaac and his whole tray full of food went down hard. Everybody laughed. And I lost it. I grabbed the kid who tripped Isaac and slammed him on the table, and I might've beaten him beyond recognition if not for the teachers who dove in and broke it up. I was so mad, I didn't care what the consequences were. Isaac didn't deserve that. Nobody could do that to him—not on my watch. That kid and everybody else in that cafeteria needed to know it.

A teacher who cared about my wrestling performance pulled me into the hallway. "If you get suspended," she said, "it will be three days out, and you won't be able to wrestle in the tournament."

That would have killed my chances to make it to states.

"I don't care!" I yelled. "Did you see that? Did you see that kid trip him?" My blood was boiling. "And you think I'm the one who should get in trouble? This is bullsh-t!" That's when the teacher hauled off and slapped me upside my face.

I felt totally justified in coming to Isaac's defense. But that slap was a wake-up call. When I looked back into my teacher's eyes, I realized something. I don't think she slapped me just because I swore at her or was disrespectful. I think she was trying to help me realize there were potential consequences to my actions.

I always had to learn the hard way.

Luckily, they let me off without a punishment. For some reason, they didn't suspend me. They let me wrestle. I knew I was lucky, though, and that I might suffer a whole lot more than a slap in the face if I ever pulled something like that again on school property.

I wrestled the whole rest of that year, and all of my movie watching and visualization and training and dreaming paid off. When we got to the end of the season, I came in as the number-nine underdog and beat out all of those higher-ranked wrestlers. I did what no one else in my county had ever done: I won the high school state championship as a freshman.

In our small town, that was a big deal. I got my picture in the paper. Everyone seemed to be talking about me. Coach Toukonen started hearing his prediction echoed all over town: "Cody's gonna be the first four-timer!"

I was so pumped about it all that I rode my bike up the street to my buddy Matt Cranmer's house and had him give me another tattoo. I didn't have my mother's permission for this one. I just went for it. Matt's a super-talented artist, and I wanted a portrait of some sort. I couldn't think of a more poignant portrait to put on my body than a portrait of Jesus. So a cross was my first tattoo, and Jesus on the cross was my second—prominently placed on my left shoulder and bicep. It was a reflection of the faith that Uncle Bob had helped bring into my life, which was present in everything I did.

I didn't want to stop winning after wrestling season was over. I wanted to box. So Uncle Bob and I both convinced my mother that I had what it took to not get my head knocked off in the ring, and she finally agreed that it was okay for me to box under Bob's supervision. I took my first amateur boxing match just before school ended my freshman year. I was fifteen years old and dressed in a pair of American flag shorts, just like the ones Apollo Creed wore in *Rocky IV*. I walked into the ring with the same mentality I always had going into a street fight—as if it were life or death, do or die—and I won that first fight with a knockout.

I won a couple more fights before wrestling season started again that fall, all under the guidance of Uncle Bob and with the blessings of my family. So later that year I got the word *family* tattooed on the inside of my arm, and then the word *relentless* because I saw myself as relentless on the wrestling mat and in the boxing ring. Getting tattoos became a bit of an addiction, I guess, and I just kept adding them. My mom would roll her eyes every time I came home with something new. She tried to encourage me to keep them in places that could be covered by a shirt so I could still get a good job someday. That was kind of funny given the fact that every adult male in our family was tattooed up like crazy. I pretty much ignored her advice, and her worry.

⁘⁘

The idea that I was going to be a four-time state champion in wrestling was a lot of pressure to put on top of all of the other pressures a young high-schooler faces. In fact, I'm pretty sure I was still a freshman the first time someone offered me drugs. Another wrestler brought some pot to a wrestling camp, and since we were all so close, we all tried it together one night. Of course we got caught and yelled at, and we promised not to do it ever again. But this was the 922. It wasn't long before pot and lots of other stuff was everywhere, ready for the taking.

I didn't do much but experiment at that time. I had my Uncle Bob's voice in my head, and I didn't want to blow my chances to be the first-ever four-timer in the state. But even without the influence of drugs, the pressure and my cockiness and my own health problems got the better of me my sophomore year. I'm not sure if I was ever actually diagnosed with mono, but I felt like I was dragging my body out of bed every day. I couldn't train right. I couldn't wrestle right. I missed a ton of school. I only got eighteen wrestling matches in the whole season.

Despite all of that, I used every bit of motivation I could muster and I kept getting back on the mat. Whenever I'd get down or tired, I'd hear the voice of that state championship announcer in my ears again, calling my name. I kept writing "Sophomore State Champion Cody Garbrandt" and "Four-Time State Champion Cody Garbrandt" on my notebooks. I might have even etched those headlines into a desk or two at school. I never gave up on my vision, and eventually all that motivational work paid off.

As the championship approached that year, I started to regain my strength. And when we were finally there, in that arena full of people, I fed off the energy of the crowd and knocked off opponents left and right. I began to feel like my old self. I got all the way to the final round again, where I wound up facing the very same kid I'd beat out to win the championship the year before.

It was epic. A real showdown.

We were down on the mat in the Schottenstein Center, surrounded by eighteen thousand fans in a back-and-forth, high-paced matchup as we both tried to establish dominance and get the first points on the board. He took me down in the first round, so I was losing two-nothing going into the second. I kept up my relentless attack, taking him out of bounds—but the pressure of the whole year seemed to catch up with me all at once. He stopped one of my shots and did a step-over bundle, wrapping my arms up and sticking me to the mat. He pinned me, and the crowd went wild.

This time, *he* was the underdog. He was out there looking for the comeback, and the crowd ate it up.

I was defeated.

I was the runner-up at states, which is a massive accomplishment, but to me it felt like the biggest loss I'd ever suffered. This wasn't just a tournament loss. This was the loss of my shot at going four for four. It was the definitive end to a dream I'd held since before I started high school.

As I came off the mat and headed toward the back of the Schottenstein Center, my assistant coach, Eric Seibert, was really cool about it. "Hey," he said, "now the stress is off of being a four-timer, you know?" When he said that, I actually felt a little bit of a relief. It had been a lot of pressure, more pressure than I even realized. So I said, "Yeah, I'll rest up, get healthy, get a good season next year." I loved his positive attitude, and I wanted to carry that attitude myself.

As we walked back toward the locker room, though, I spotted Coach Toukonen. He was sort of pacing back and forth. I could tell something was wrong. He looked at me sort of scornfully and said, "Ah, I just really wanted you to be my first four-time state champion."

I was taken aback by that, like, "Whoa." I kind of understood where he was coming from. This was his shot, too, and he must've thought, *Oh man, I'm almost there!* But the way he put it really bothered me: "*My* first four-time state champion."

Like I said, this was somebody I looked up to almost as a father figure. I couldn't help but wonder, *Was this about me, or was this about* your *goal?*

I said back to him, "You don't think I wanted to be a four-time state champ, Coach? I literally dedicated every day of my life to this!" He knew that. He knew I'd dedicated myself to this sport since I was a little kid. He knew it was what I'd always wanted to do. Now here I was only a few minutes past getting beat in front of eighteen thousand people, and I was upset, and that's all he had to say?

I've never spoken about this publicly before, but that moment was the reason I quit wrestling. It wasn't because I lost the championship and got down on myself, which is what most people assumed. I would've loved to go back the next year and prove I could beat that guy who pinned me or anyone else who took his place. But the way Coach looked at me in that tunnel on the way out of the Schottenstein Center, the way he spoke to me—that hurt.

I don't mean to get down on Coach Toukonen. I don't. The man taught me a lot. He's a great coach with an amazing legacy that deserves to be celebrated. And maybe I took his demeanor all wrong. I just know what it felt like at the time.

The way he spoke to me in that moment made it seem like he'd lost faith in me, when what I really wanted, and what I really needed, was to know that Coach had my back.

Uncle Bob had my back.

No sooner did I lose my passion for wrestling than he stepped in to pump up my passion for boxing. He threw me back in the gym and started me working on the heavy bag, and suddenly all of the focus I'd thrown into wrestling for the past two years came rushing into my two hands.

I couldn't get enough. I fought fifteen fights in the tristate region (Kentucky, Ohio, and West Virginia) that one summer after my sophomore year. And Uncle Bob kept pushing me. There were times we would go fight Friday in Ohio, Saturday in Pennsylvania, and West Virginia on Sunday. It was exhausting. Every once in a while I'd complain about it: "Man, we're fighting three times in a row!" And Bob would be like, "I remember when we fought four times in one day."

"Well, that was back in the day, man," I'd say. "You're hella punch-drunk!"

I wasn't really complaining. I loved every second of it. Every bit of passion I'd lost for wrestling I had found again—and then some—with boxing and Uncle Bob. This was me and my uncle, who I loved and looked up to, and no matter how hard we worked at it, we'd always have fun. We would shed blood, sweat, and tears in the gym, then we'd go out there against some other team that wanted it almost as bad, and that blood between us gave us an edge.

I felt like a Roman Gladiator going into battle for the honor of my family. I fell in love with those types of movies too. *Gladiator*, *Troy*, and *Braveheart*. I felt like a warrior every time I stepped into the ring.

The great fighter Arturo "Thunder" Gati was my inspiration from the boxing world, and I took his nickname as my own: Cody "Thunder" Garbrandt. I pulled from Coach Toukonen's playbook and had the venues play AC/DC's "Thunderstruck" as my walkout music before every fight.

Getting to those venues wasn't easy. I was scared to death to fly, which meant I sometimes had to be driven long distances to fight. I didn't even have my license, and yet I had the backing from my family to go fight all over the country if I wanted.

Man, that's what you want in life. You want people to back you up and be proud of you when you're happy and pursuing your passion. That's everything, right there.

Boxing wasn't like wrestling, though. There were no massive arenas or state championships to be had at the high school amateur level. So I didn't have as clear-cut a goal as I'd had back when I set my sights on the wrestling wins. I didn't have an announcer's voice in my ear, other than the ones I heard on TV. I couldn't visualize the crowd or hear them roar, except when I watched fights on TV between grown-up professional fighters. I loved boxing—don't get me wrong. I just couldn't see a clear path to greatness in the sport.

I think Uncle Bob saw a path for me. He didn't even want me to try out for the Olympic team the way he had. He thought right from the start that I could go pro. After every fight he would say, "Man, ten more fights like that and you'll go pro! Ten more fights!"

He wasn't over the top about it. He wasn't like somebody's stage mom, trying to live out their dreams through their kid. He just wanted to see me be the best I could be—for me. Which means he didn't necessarily care if I won or lost. He cared that I fought hard, gave it everything I could. And if I lost— *when* I lost—he cared that I learned from my mistakes and fought better the next time because of them.

I always did.

I didn't seem to be very good at learning lessons outside of the ring, though. Instead of keeping my head down and staying out of trouble while I focused on school and boxing, I started running with a reckless crowd. We'd wind up at these big parties almost every weekend, and inevitably a fight would break out. My friends and I would beat some guys up, and then next thing we knew they'd go out, round up *their* friends, and come back with weapons.

I remember being in the middle of a thirty-man brawl at one party, with people getting messed up all around me. One guy started swinging a heavy metal chain, cracking people in the head. My quickness in the ring from all my training with Uncle Bob was the only reason I didn't get knocked in the head by that chain myself. There were bodies all over. Another time I watched one of my buddies get hit in the head with a crowbar.

So even though things were going so good with me in the boxing world, I kept winding up right on the edge of losing it all. Think about it: I just missed getting hit in the head with the chain. What if I'd been looking the other way? It wasn't my head that got split open with the crowbar, but it was the head of my buddy, who was right next to me!

In the light of day, after all of that went down and I dragged myself out of bed to go running at five in the morning or to go to church with Uncle Bob, I'd think about it. I'd step back and say, "Man, that was a little too close."

Then I'd go out and do it again.

One time, right between my sophomore and junior years, an adult from our neighborhood who'd just gotten out of prison picked a fight with me and my friends in the park. I don't know if he was drunk or what, but he started talking sh-t to us while we were playing basketball, and my buddy ended up breaking his hand when they went at it. So I stepped in and beat the guy down. But when he made his way back to his car, he pulled out a gun. If one of my other friends hadn't wrestled it away from him real quick, who knows what might have happened. Luckily, he didn't come back later with another gun for revenge. But he could have.

Over and over again, these near misses kept happening.

The guys around me bragged about the whole thing. They liked living on the edge. But in my mind, especially on those Sunday mornings, I'd be like, *Wow, the adrenaline rush of it was awesome, but that was a close call.*

I knew I wanted more for myself. I knew I wanted to be a professional fighter. But it was really hard to separate myself from that life. I didn't know any other life, and it was all amped up because of the crew that I hung out with. A lot of them sold drugs. A lot of them did drugs too. I didn't dabble in it hardly at all. I didn't like the way it felt when my body was out of my control. Plus, my father and uncles did that. I didn't want that for myself.

Uncle Bob was always on me when I got too close to the edge. He'd look at my bruised-up face in the morning and see I hadn't slept. "Cody, you never win on drugs," he'd say. "Nobody wins on drugs." I knew he was telling the truth.

But the fighting? I just couldn't escape the fact that it was a way of life in the 922. It seemed like every few days either I or somebody I knew would get called out to go fight down at the pump house.

The pump house was this old water-treatment building on the outskirts of town, next to a little river. Not many cars drove by there, and the cops never seemed to be around. So it became the go-to spot where people would go to settle their scores. There was barely four feet between the pull-off and the river, so the fights and the crowds that would gather to watch usually spilled right out into the street.

Zach and I took to fighting each other at the pump house in our teen years too. When we were at our grandparents' house, which was less than a mile from that spot, our grandparents just wouldn't put up with our fighting anymore. We were big by then. We'd wind up breaking furniture if we stayed inside. So they'd kick us out, and Zach would take off in his pickup truck, saying the fight was over, and I'd chase after him and jump in the back of the truck. I never wanted to let it go. So he'd pull into the pump house and get out, and we'd finish fighting there. We wouldn't even say a word. We'd just get out of the truck and start fighting again.

Zach always won. He was the only guy who could ever beat me up, and he beat me up relentlessly. I don't know why I was so hardheaded about it, but I would not let him walk away until he put me on the ground. With my wrestling dreams gone and my boxing dreams unfocused, Zach was the one I had to answer to. Like I said, he'd always been bigger than me and stronger than me, and that was never so clear as in those final years of high school. My brother was my toughest opponent, bar none.

FOUR

I WAS TWELVE YEARS OLD THE FIRST TIME I SAW A
mixed martial arts fight on TV. I was in a hotel room with a few other kids up
in Illinois getting ready for a big wrestling tournament—and I couldn't take
my eyes off the screen.

Here were two guys in a cage—squared up, boxing, but with nothing but
a set of light grappling gloves on their hands and their thumbs sticking out.
No body pads. No escape. All of a sudden they were in a hold, but no ref broke
them up. One guy took the other down, and suddenly they were wrestling—
and again, no one stopped them. The other guy broke free and popped back
up, and when the first guy came at him he threw a kick!

"What was that?!" I yelled right out loud. "Is that even allowed?"

"Yeah, bro," one of the other kids said. "It's MMA. Mixed martial arts.
You can do everything!"

It *was* everything. It looked like a street brawl, but I could tell it wasn't.
These guys were disciplined. The wrestling was good. The boxing was good.
The kicks—well, I didn't know much about kicks. My mom had never had
enough money to put us into karate lessons, and what I saw of martial arts
classes in the area seemed a little lame to me. Those white outfits and the
colored belts and the lack of contact in most classes—I just didn't get it. But
these guys made it look cool.

I convinced the whole wrestling team to bring their mattresses into our
hotel room and stand them up against the walls. We turned that room into

our own padded cage, where I challenged everyone to fight me MMA style. Everyone—the heavyweights, the lightweights, the older kids, I didn't care. I was so pumped up about the idea of combining everything I knew about boxing and wrestling into the same sport that I just wanted to see how it felt to actually do it.

Needless to say, it felt great.

Even the bigger kids were surprised at how strong my punches were. They didn't know I'd been training to box with Uncle Bob on the side. And after my punches threw them off guard, they were surprised by the fact that a little guy like me could take them down so fast. I was good at MMA! I didn't even really need to test myself in that hotel room to know that, either. I knew it the moment I watched that fight on TV. I could see myself in that cage, in what they called the octagon—arms raised, a championship belt around my waist. I could hear the crowd. I could feel what it felt like to win.

I asked Uncle Bob what he thought of the sport. "Cage fighting?" he said. "No, dude. There's no future in that. You want to be a millionaire? Boxing's where it's at."

It was the same old line, the same old thing he'd been telling Zach and me since we were little kids. And I believed him. I didn't know the names of any MMA fighters. They weren't the heroes people looked up to. And there weren't any movies about MMA fighters in those days. It was just fun to watch on TV.

I was sure I wanted to try it at some point. But where did someone go to get into MMA fighting anyway? There weren't any gyms where I lived, no fights that I knew of, no circuit. I'd never even seen a cage match in real life. So I quickly put any thoughts of becoming an MMA fighter to the side.

MMA wouldn't leave me alone, though. Over the next few years, the sport gained in popularity, and local fights did pop up. Some bar somewhere would bring a cage into their parking lot on the weekend and sell tickets. I made Uncle Bob drive me to every fight we could find. I loved watching those fights and picturing myself in the cage. I was a scrappy fighter, man, and the idea of getting paid to get scrappy in every way I knew how was exciting to me.

By the time I was in high school, I did know the names of some MMA fighters. Chuck Liddell and Tito Ortiz were becoming superstars and getting on the covers of magazines. Even people who didn't watch the sport knew those guys by name. People were talking about MMA. It seemed like a sport on the rise, and there was no question that the Ultimate Fighting Championship was the top of the game. UFC events were held in big arenas in places like Las Vegas, and who could ever forget the voices of announcer Bruce Buffer and his half-brother Michael, who trademarked the catchphrase, "Let's get ready to rumble!" I got the sound of those voices in my head the same way I got the sound of the announcers at the Schottenstein in my head as a kid. I could hear them calling out my name. Every time I watched a fight on TV, I had visions of UFC president Dana White strapping that big gold championship belt around my waist. I couldn't get it out of my head.

Most of the big names in the UFC in those days were heavyweights, just like in old-school boxing. For some reason the big guys draw the most attention. But I learned the names of some smaller guys, too—the guys who were built more like me—and I was absolutely blown away by the fighting of a guy named Urijah Faber.

Faber wasn't a part of the UFC when I first caught wind of him in the mid-2000s. He was fighting in the Gladiator Challenge and for World Extreme Cagefighting (WEC). But he was a killer. He was so aggressive in the octagon. He fought the way I wanted to fight, so I read everything I could find about him. He had a wrestling background, just like me, and he was five-foot-six, just like me, but he had also studied Brazilian jiu-jitsu. (I made a mental note to myself that I needed to take martial arts much more seriously.) He was this good-looking blond California dude who seemed to get all sorts of attention from women, but the greatest thing he did was draw attention to the bantamweight division of the sport, which is right where I'd wind up fitting in if I ever made it to the UFC myself.

This was right around the time a new thing called YouTube was starting to take off, which meant I suddenly had access to uploaded videos of fights and could watch whenever I wanted. I watched some of Urijah's fights over and over and over just to analyze what he was doing and to figure out how to do it myself.

I basically did all of this on the side, of course, because after I'd given up on wrestling, Uncle Bob kept trying to convince me that boxing was the only way to go. He wanted me to stay focused. He saw that I was a good boxer, that I had promise. And I listened to him. I believed in him as a coach, a mentor, a father figure—all of it. How could I not? He'd dedicated so much of his life to me. And even in that first summer after my sophomore year, in my first fifteen boxing matches, the value of his coaching had shown itself to be superior. I seemed to walk right over just about anybody I faced in the ring, and I knew that what I'd learned from my uncle was a huge part of the secret to my success.

Uncle Bob and his old boxing trainer, Chris Fury, came up with something they called "the Numbers," a series of sequenced moves in the ring that he believed would give a boxer an edge in any fight and against any opponent. These sequences were really about fundamentals, working your stance and your footwork, but he'd drilled them down into a really complex system that's difficult for others to visualize, let alone grasp. It's even difficult to explain.

The closest thing I can think of are the forms or katas you might learn in a karate class—the intricate routines of movement, steps, and turns that karate students aim to perfect. Only Uncle Bob's Numbers aren't done in slow motion, and they aren't focused on the form and balance of the movement as some sort of dance. They're focused on the speed and power of what can be accomplished in an actual fight.

There are twenty-something Numbers in all, each one more complex than the other. The whole system was so complicated that Zach gave it up after getting to Number 7. But I took to this system like a natural. I just got it. It made sense to me. And I was developing the speed and athleticism to pull off all the sequences Uncle Bob had long envisioned in his mind.

We actually started working on the Numbers the first time Uncle Bob took me and Zach to meet Chris Fury. I was so little back then that I couldn't even hold the gloves up. Those sixteen-ounce gloves were too much for me. But I heard Chris and Bob say that squaring up like you do in a street fight, with your full body facing forward and both of your hands up, is stupid. It leaves you too vulnerable. It's important to stand at an angle, so you've always got an angle on your opponent. And the thing a lot of people miss about that stance is that when you step, "you always want to step to the outside of your foot, so you've always got that angle," Bob said.

To help us accomplish that, he started walking us through the Numbers. So there's Number 1, which is basically one punch and a step to back it up and keep the angle. Then there's Number 2, a one-two sequence with a second punch following up from the angle you've cut with the Number 1 step. And then there's the straight 3, which is jab, right, jab. But there's a variation on that 3, which is jab, right hook, jab. And 4—the one I really took to when I was fifteen and started boxing for real—is jab, right hook, overhand right, and then duck the head.

I pretty much perfected that Number-4 sequence early on, and my opponents rarely saw it coming. It seemed that not many fighters did two right-hand punches in a row, and so not many fighters expected it. People expect a right to be followed by a left and a left to be followed by a right. That's just the natural way most people fight. So that right hook, overhand right sequence came off as some sort of superhuman talent to some people. But all it was, really, was Uncle Bob's system, his Numbers, which I practiced over and over again.

After 4, the Numbers got even more complicated. And as I got a little older and faster, I noticed that other guys in the gym just couldn't keep up with what I was doing.

I can't explain how Uncle Bob put it all together in his mind. It's just his talent—a God-given gift, maybe. A dream he never gave up. He knew his Numbers would work in the hands of a great fighter. And I'm pretty sure he started to see me as the fighter who could pull it off.

Even with the Numbers system proving itself to be a winner, giving me an edge not only in the ring but in street fights, too, I kept dreaming about climbing into a cage and putting all of my skills to the test—as a wrestler, a boxer, and the street fighter I always was. In casual fights with friends I found myself throwing kicks, just to try them out.

Legally I wouldn't be eligible to fight MMA, even on an amateur level, until I was eighteen years old. That drove me nuts. I wanted it so bad, and I hated waiting. So I talked about it all the time.

Of course, my talking about wanting to make it as an MMA fighter was met with all kinds of negativity from other people, the same way people had been negative about me wanting to become a wrestler and even a boxer. I loved to fight, but I was constantly told I would "never amount to nothing" in fighting. I was too small. I was too this or too that. And then there was the old, "Fighting's not going to get you anywhere but in prison with your father."

Loving to fight and learning how to do it better was my passion. So it wasn't easy to hear my teachers, my coaches, and sometimes my friends or my friends' parents say things like, "Why would you want to do that? Why do you want to fight? Just go to college."

Sometimes I wrestled with whether or not I was wrong to keep dreaming. I had all of those people in my ear telling me I was wrong, telling me to go to school, get a good-paying job in one of the coal mines, or do something else that would be "better" for me. Safer. Easier. But I always wanted to fight. And when I found the UFC, I was like, "That's my American dream."

Down in my gut, I knew I wanted more than just boxing, more than just wrestling. I didn't want to focus on just one thing when I could combine everything. I didn't understand why people were so restrictive in their thinking. Why couldn't I participate in multiple sports at once? More important, why couldn't I combine multiple sports into one? Why did everything have to follow such a straight line?

When my junior year came around, I decided to join my brother on the high school football field. I needed to fill up my time while I waited to go after the one thing I wanted, and I thought it would be fun to play football like we used to when we were younger. So I threw everything I had into football. I focused. I practiced hard. I worked out hard. I followed Zach's lead in the gym, where he'd push me to the limit, telling me to "make the walls sweat!" And I did.

I came back to football after what felt like forever, and just a few weeks into the season I scored five touchdowns in a single game—tying the state record.

Playing football didn't make me any more disciplined off the field, though. It seemed like nothing could do that. It felt like I faced a constant battle in my life, a pull between two lives and two sets of values. I went to church on

Sundays and said my prayers, but I kept getting into fights and kept running with my crew. I needed money and didn't have time for a regular job between football practice and boxing workouts, so I joined my friends and wound up selling drugs now and then just to make some money. It was easy. It was available. It was all right there at any moment.

Life was one big emotional roller coaster, but I guess that's why life and fighting go hand in hand for me. You never know what's going to happen next in a fight. You work hard, and you go in there having supreme confidence in your training, but some guy can come in there and knock you the hell out. You've just got to be aware of that possibility and not let it knock you out for good.

I only have one explanation for why the darker side of my life didn't consume me the way it did a lot of other kids—my dreams. I dreamed of making it as a wrestler, then as a boxer, and then as an MMA fighter. Those dreams are what kept me going, and they always managed to pull me back from trouble, even when I didn't expect them to. They would just pop into my mind throughout my day. Even when I was partying and getting all messed up, or messing around with some girl, I'd get a flash of myself standing in the octagon, the lights all around me, the crowd roaring. I'd be right in the middle of getting up to no good when I'd see that dream and taste it for a moment and think, *Dude, this isn't what you're supposed to be doing.*

It would hit me like a flash.

I would get hit with a sense of guilt.

Sometimes I would react poorly to the guilt and try to cover it up with even more alcohol or drugs. But sometimes that flash was strong enough to stop me. I'd cool things down with the girl I was with. I'd say no to the cocaine somebody was offering. I'd put down my drink. I'd leave the party. In retrospect, I thank the Lord for that vision. I thank the Lord for that dream. Because I know with absolute certainty that if the Lord hadn't placed it inside my heart, I might have wound up in prison or dead. I know that was my alternate fate. I know it.

So many people don't even dare to dream, you know? They stop dreaming because of some fear they have or because of all the doubters who try to stop them. And honestly, given my circumstances, there is no one to thank but God for keeping my dream alive during my high school years.

⚍

I knew I would finally be able to step into the octagon after my junior year. I wanted to be ready. I wanted to jump into the cage the moment I turned eighteen, and that meant I needed to spend the rest of my junior year training.

I knew my wrestling game was strong, even though I wasn't wrestling on the high school team anymore. I knew my boxing game was strong because Uncle Bob was taking me deeper into the fundamentals, the sweet science of boxing, every time we got together, and I kept proving myself in the ring on weekends. In fact, I was so relentless in the ring, Uncle Bob started making comments about it: "Cody, you show no love to your opponents. No love!"

It was true. I was ruthless. And it didn't take long before Uncle Bob's description of me became the full-blown nickname that follows me to this day. I became Cody "No Love" Garbrandt.

But I needed to learn more. I needed to learn some martial arts, and I needed to learn the ins and outs of combining all those skills in the best way possible to bring down opponents in the cage. I needed a coach who believed in the future of MMA fighting. And as luck would have it, I was able to find one right in between my old town and my new high school.

Brian Cadle's Main Street Gym in Roswell, Ohio, wasn't much of a gym. It was a woodshop in a barn that just happened to have enough room for some mats and a boxing ring off to one side. But it was all I needed.

There was something gritty about the place that I liked. It reminded me of the farmhouse in *Rocky IV* where Rocky went to train before his match against Russian powerhouse Ivan Drago. No frills. No fancy equipment. Just weights and bags and a place to get away from the world to concentrate on what mattered.

There was no air conditioning, so in the summer the place got brutally hot. And in the winter, the only heat was from a propane burner that stank up the place and made it hard to breathe. We had to choose between breathing and freezing sometimes. But Brian was a great guy with a love for the MMA world, and he wanted to build that woodshop into a real MMA gym. He welcomed Uncle Bob and me with open arms, since we brought some additional boxing and wrestling cred to bolster what he'd already developed.

Word got around that the two of us were training in that spot, and suddenly we drew in a whole crew of boxers and wrestlers from the area who wanted to transition to MMA too. We were all dead set on grinding it out and figuring it out on our own, firmly believing that our style of brutal hand-to-hand training would be rougher and tougher than anything our opponents could ever throw at us in the cage.

Throwing myself into MMA training during my downtime kept me out of trouble. Between school and that, there just wasn't much time left to go running with my old crew. But those workouts also helped me keep my head on straight. Throwing myself into training, knowing that the clock was ticking and that I'd find myself in the octagon shortly after the end of that school year, gave every day a purpose.

It would have been so easy to go the other way. I was clearly a person who did things full-on. And I could have been that way as a partier or drug dealer—going at it full throttle until the wheels fell off. But somehow God gave me the power to choose something else and surrounded me with mentors and family members—even as messed up as my family could be—who helped me.

When summer finally came, I was ready.

Brian Cadle, who'd become a friend, a coach, and even a benefactor for me—he'd stepped up and paid to renew my boxing license when I didn't have the money to pay for it—set me up with my first MMA fight just two and a half weeks after my eighteenth birthday. It was a pretty huge fight too—part of an NAAFS (North American Allied Fight Series) event called the War on the Shore 3. The outdoor, under-the-lights night fight would take place at a bar up in Geneva, Ohio, right on Lake Erie.

Driving into the parking lot and seeing that cage under the lights was a dream come true for me. I was about to step into everything I'd wanted and visualized for all those years. I wasn't nervous. I was just excited. Excited to get started. Excited to win.

As soon as we got out of the car, though, everything seemed to go wrong. When I went to change, I couldn't find my fight shorts. Brian had to buy me a new pair on-site, and they were a little too big, which meant that I had to pull the drawstring really tight around my waist.

Those shorts weren't comfortable at all. They weren't what I was used to. But whatever. I wasn't going to let that throw me off. I just wanted to lay eyes on my opponent at weigh-in and start sizing him up. Only my opponent, a guy named Nick Hyatt who had lost his first and only amateur fight a month earlier, didn't show up for weigh-in. He just plain wasn't there.

I was pacing around, wondering if Hyatt was even going to show up, when the skies opened up. It started pouring rain. Then it seemed like everything went real fast. Next thing I knew, they were wrapping my gloves and saying it was time.

I made my way up to the cage. The floor of the octagon was soaking wet and slippery as I stepped in. I wasn't even sure if my opponent had weighed in at all, and when I finally saw him, I noticed he was taller than me. I barely had time to size him up before we were going at it, with the lights glaring off the rain-soaked floor and my bare feet slipping beneath me every time I took a step.

I started off well. I hit him with a three-piece combo and dropped him. *Boom.* But then he hooked my leg and scrambled toward the cage. I'd read that he was a good Division 1 wrestler, and he showed those skills pretty quick, but I held my own until he grabbed onto the cage itself and wouldn't let go. I tried to lift him, and the ref kept telling him, "Let go of the cage! Let go of the cage!"

Finally the ref reached over and knocked Hyatt's hand free. Hyatt slipped down to the floor, and that sent me totally off balance. In the shift, just two minutes into the first round, Hyatt managed to catch me in a naked choke hold. I'm not even sure how he did it. I couldn't get a foot planted to gain any leverage at all.

I hadn't done much training in jiu-jitsu at that point, and between the slippery floor and my lack of skills, I couldn't get free. He had me. I felt myself blacking out. I had no choice. At 2:06 in my first-ever MMA fight, I tapped out.

I surrendered.

I lost.

FIVE

IN THE CAR ON THE WAY HOME FROM GENEVA, Brian Cadle looked at me and said, "Man, someday you're gonna laugh about this. Trust me—you're gonna laugh about it."

I tried to laugh about it right then and there, but I couldn't. That loss stung.

I hated losing even more than I loved winning. Losing was the worst feeling in the world. It didn't matter if Zach and I were racing to see who could get to the shower first and he managed to slam the door shut in my face or if I was getting pinned in front of eighteen thousand people at the Schottenstein Center—to me, it was all the same. I hated it.

In the wake of losing my first MMA fight, I thought about Rocky. I thought about Rudy. I thought about the warriors in all of those great movies I loved. They all suffered defeat at some point. They all got knocked down. And I was well aware of the big, loud message that every one of those great stories delivered: winning isn't about how many times you get knocked down; it's about how many times you get back up. Still, it sure is hard to think motivational thoughts when you're flat on the ground. And I felt like I was on the ground for sure.

Brian kept making the point that the fight had been nothing but a comedy of errors, with my oversized shorts and the rain and the ref knocking my opponent's hand off the cage. I mean, really, it was just a stupid fight in the parking lot of some bar. For all the hype, it was nothing compared to where I wanted to be. The UFC. Las Vegas. Fighting like my man Urijah Faber. On top of the world.

I hoped that someday he'd be right.

Once we were back home, I tried to pump myself up a bit. I got back to the gym the very next day. I knew I was better than the results of that first fight. I knew I had what it took to be great. I knew I was willing to put in the work. Because I was still in school, though, that work would have to be put off for a while.

I started playing high school football again that fall—and taking out my fighting aggressions in old-school street fights.

The lesson I should have learned after jumping to Isaac's defense in the cafeteria in my freshman year didn't stick for some reason. It's like I needed to get hit over the head with it again and again and again. It didn't occur to me at the time, but getting into fights outside of the ring was always a choice, and the consequences of those fights affected my football games and everything else.

Sometimes I'd get injured off the field and have to sit out a game. But instead of waking up and thinking, *gee, maybe I shouldn't do that—maybe I should walk away next time*, I was stupid about it. I didn't care. "At least I won the fight," I'd tell myself.

The words of my coaches were enough to pull me back on track most of the time—words like, "There's nothing worse than seeing wasted talent." I didn't want to be some coach's negative example. But I still came face-to-face with hard choices every day, and I didn't always choose wisely.

Finally, one of those fights beat me up.

Our football team didn't have a lot of discipline. We certainly weren't an elite program, and we all acted like idiots when no one was watching. So I wound up getting into it more than once with the other players in the locker room. That fall, one of my teammate's moms decided to make a fuss about it. I guess I hurt her kid, and she decided to make me pay. The lady filled out some sort of official report, which meant the principal couldn't shake his head and walk away from this one. The consequences fell, and fell hard.

They kicked me out of school.

Coincidentally, Zach got kicked out of school right around the same time. He had just become the first member of our family to get into college—on a full-boat wrestling scholarship, no less—only to get kicked out and thrown in jail for getting into a brutal fight during his very first semester.

Zach and I were definitely cut from the same cloth.

I couldn't help but wonder sometimes if both of our fates were sealed. What if there was nothing we could do to stop ourselves from following in our father's footsteps? It's hard to have something like that hanging over you while you're trying to go about your life and achieve your dreams.

As it turned out, though, getting kicked out of Claymont High School was a good thing for me. I was angry about it, of course. I didn't think it was fair. But I wound up transferring a couple of towns over to New Philadelphia that fall of my senior year. New Philadelphia had a serious football program. We're talking a coach who'd been there for years, who believed in building a program while building up his players. He was the kind of guy who'd gather the team to watch tape of the practices and games, analyze the details of the plays, and get the whole team to focus on getting better together as a unit.

This coach at New Philadelphia, Coach Dennison, had strict rules too. Like, he made me and the others keep a clean-cut, totally shaven face. No beards. No facial hair at all. I'd been wearing one kind of beard or another since eighth grade, so it was shocking to have to shave it off, but it was just a thing with him. If you broke the rule, you couldn't play. And I wanted to play.

He also made us dress up and wear ties to and from the locker room on game day. He drilled us over and over again on the idea of showing respect— respect for our teammates, respect for our opponents, respect for our school, respect for our fans, respect for ourselves.

It worked. It felt awesome to go out there and play knowing that I had the actual support of my teammates rather than constantly getting into fights with them and bucking up against rivalries on our own side of the field. We went out there and won again and again—not because of one superstar, not because a Cody or a Zach or someone like us scored five touchdowns, but because we all worked hard together.

It was almost surreal. Just being at a different school during the day, spending most of my time just a few miles away from my regular crew and the same old same old of our little twin cities, somehow opened up all sorts of new possibilities for me.

My experience on the football team at New Philadelphia was so good, I decided to give wrestling another go as well. But the wrestling program there wasn't as good as my old team back home. So we got my old school to take me back.

Once I was back at Claymont High, I found out I was ineligible for wrestling because I'd made an in-season transfer. That left a lot of time on my hands—time that I seemed to constantly split between partying and trying to refocus on MMA fighting.

When Zach got out of prison and moved back home, we hung out. He came over and trained with me and Uncle Bob and Brian Cadle at Main Street Gym. It was just like old times. And one night while visiting our grandparents, the two of us got into a fight.

It started over a Subway chicken sandwich. I was getting ready for what turned out to be one of my last amateur boxing matches, and I was watching my weight, so I ate half the sandwich before I went to work out and left the other half in my grandparents' fridge to finish later. But I got back from the gym to find that Zach had eaten my sandwich—and he started laughing about it.

That laugh set off a rage in me. I tackled him out of his seat in the living room, and we wrestled hard, knocking into the table and smashing a lamp to the floor. In the split second that I looked away, thinking how mad that was gonna make our grandpa, Zach picked me up and slammed me down head-first into the floor. I nearly blacked out.

"Take it outside!" Grandpa yelled.

At that point Zach just left, thinking he'd won the fight. He hopped in his truck and took off. But I shook it off, ran outside, hopped into my pickup truck, and followed him.

Then, just like old times, we pulled off at the pump house and went at it.

Despite Zach's size, we were clearly more evenly matched than ever before. He would hit me and knock me back, then I'd come back and hit him and knock him back. We kept at it like that, giving everything we had in the glare of our headlights, for a solid forty-five minutes. Six or seven cars came down that dark road, forcing us to stop and move out of the way each time. But every time we stopped, we caught our breath and just started it up again right after.

"F-ck you!" I yelled at one point. "I'm gonna knock you out and throw you in the river!"

We were pretty deep into it when I pulled a variation of Number 4 and caught Zach with a one-two punch followed by an overhand right that connected with his jaw.

That's when I saw something in Zach's eyes I hadn't seen since back when we fought in the woods in preschool and I split his head open with a stick. Zach was hurt. His knees buckled, and he almost went down.

I backed off and just stood there, staring at him. I'd never bested him like that before. I'd never seriously hurt him with my bare hands.

While I stood there in disbelief, realizing that this was a moment I'd dreamed of—the moment when I could finally say that I beat my big brother, when I finally proved I was the better fighter—Zach dove at me, pinned me on the ground, and started pounding the right side of my head. He ripped my ear to shreds.

"Stop!" I yelled. "Stop!" He finally looked at me through his rage and saw all of the blood, and he pulled back.

As he started to stand, I hooked him with my heel, pulled him down, and punched him square in the nose.

"You little prick!" he yelled, and we were right back at it, both of us soaked in our own blood. Only something unspoken had changed, and we both knew it. In the next few minutes, our punches slowed. We backed off of each other. We cooled down. We kept falling into each other like two exhausted old boxers at the end of the twelfth round. I think we both realized, somewhere deep down, that if we carried on any further, one of us was going to wind up severely hurt. Or killed.

I loved my brother. I didn't want to maim the guy. And I'd seen what Zach could do in a street fight. I'm pretty sure he didn't want to take me down and put a knee through his own brother's face. That was the only level left for us, and neither one of us wanted to go there.

We walked away and got into our trucks, then went back to our grand-parents' house and showered up. We wound up sitting at the kitchen table together grabbing a late-night snack, and we've never fought like that again.

I have carried the scar of that fight ever since in the form of my cauli-flower ear. That's right: my own brother gave me that permanent scar. But in so many ways, it was worth it.

I won that fight. I'm not sure Zach would openly admit it, but I knew I won. I knew—and he knew—that if I'd followed up with anything rather than stand there dumbfounded after his knees went wobbly, I would've knocked him out. *Boom.* It would have been lights out.

That meant something to me.

Zach wasn't planning on becoming a professional fighter. Now that his college career was over, he figured his next best move would be to take a good-paying job in a coal mine, and that's what he was getting ready to do. The training he did with us was just for fun, just to keep in shape.

But for me, this wasn't like old times anymore. This was the start of a new era—a whole new life for me. From that moment on, I didn't have my eyes set on beating up my big brother. My goals, and all of my aggression, were focused on the cage.

SIX

I ENTERED MY SECOND-EVER MMA FIGHT AS AN
amateur in April of 2010, in East Liverpool, Ohio. I fought this kid named
Ryan Rooney, a good wrestler from New Jersey, and I TKO'd him in the second round. The ref stopped the fight because I was landing so many strikes on
the guy. I just beat the piss out of him the whole fight.

A month later I set my third fight down in Zanesville, Ohio. This fight
was held at the county fairgrounds, and when I got there, I found out that
my opponent was thirty-something years old. He had his two kids there with
him, and at weigh-in, he came in over weight. The commission hesitated about
sanctioning the fight, and all the worrying and waiting while they made their
decision just made me angry. By the time we finally got in the cage, I TKO'd
him just 1:21 into the first round.

I put some video of myself winning those two fights on YouTube, right
next to some of my training videos that showed just how hard I was working
out in between fights. I was so pumped about everything that I even tweeted a
message to Urijah Faber. I'd followed his every move as he made his way to the
UFC. By then he'd founded his own gym and formed Team Alpha Male out
in Sacramento, California, and the guys on his team were awesome. I wanted
to be just like them. So while I was riding my high of back-to-back wins, I
tweeted to Urijah's Twitter account: "I hope to be out there with Team Alpha
Male in the near future."

That's when something really cool happened. Urijah Faber tweeted me back: "Hey man. Good luck. We'll be out here when you're ready."

I couldn't believe it. I was tweeting directly with my MMA hero!

I wrote back immediately: "Mark my words. I'll be out there."

A few minutes later, he tweeted back again: "I believe you. I checked out your stuff on YouTube and look forward to having you."

I was nineteen years old and just starting out, and this guy I totally respected and admired had just opened a door to the possibility that my wildest dreams weren't out of my reach. Urijah Faber had checked out my videos and "looked forward to having" me at his gym.

That was a game changer.

There was just one problem: I let myself get sidetracked.

Once I was finally eligible to wrestle again come May, I went down to Senior Nationals just to challenge myself. Even after all those months away from the sport, I still placed fifth in the nation.

Suddenly there were scouts all around, setting their sights on me and talking about college scholarships.

My mom was all excited about the possibility of me going to college. She'd loved seeing me all clean-cut and wearing a tie on New Philadelphia game days, and I think picturing me looking like that at college made her proud.

I liked making her proud. That was a good feeling. But to be honest, I wasn't real excited about the possibility of going to college at all. I didn't know anything about college other than the fact that Zach had gone—and look how that turned out. Plus, college would just mean more schoolwork, and that did not sound enticing to me.

What I really wanted to do, more than ever before, was to fight. And more specifically, to transition from boxing to MMA full time so I could make it to the UFC. That's what lit me up. But I went through the motions of filling out college applications and taking all the tests I was supposed to take anyway. I even went way outside my comfort zone and got on a plane for the very first time to go look at schools, and I accepted an offer to attend Newberry College down in South Carolina on a wrestling scholarship. I put on a cap and gown and celebrated on high school graduation day like all of the other kids, which was quite an accomplishment considering the long line of my relatives who'd never made it through high school (not counting Zach's diploma and Uncle Bob's prison schooling, of course).

But none of that stuff got me excited. None of it. All I looked forward to, all I really cared about, was getting back to fighting MMA full time. But now, instead of focusing on MMA, I was turning my attention back to wrestling and getting ready to leave for college.

College wasn't my dream. It was everybody else's dream for me. It was my mom's dream. It was my teachers' dream. Sometimes it felt like it was society's dream—like the only measure of a man is whether or not he's college educated, and those who aren't are just the so-called "lowlifes" society doesn't care about, the ones who wind up working in the coal mines and factories. I couldn't understand that mindset then, and I don't understand it now, because it's just not true. There are a million ways to get ahead in life, and college is only one of them.

Still, I wanted to make Mom happy. I wanted to make everyone happy. I had earned that wrestling scholarship, which was a big deal. So I packed up my things and headed off to South Carolina.

Three months later, I withdrew from school.

The academic side of college just wasn't for me. I didn't get along with a lot of the other students, either. I suppose I could've skated by and dealt with it all if I'd really been into wrestling, but that was the thing that really got me down: I just didn't want to wrestle anymore. It wasn't my path.

I wanted my dream.

The scariest part of making the decision to leave school was making the phone call to my mom. What if she wouldn't let me move back home? Where would I go? Without the scholarship and a dorm room, I had nowhere to live. I didn't have any money. I didn't have a job. I also just plain didn't want to disappoint her. She'd looked so proud the day I left for school.

I was surprised by how well she took the news, though. She didn't say anything about being disappointed. She just wanted me to be sure I was making the right decision, and I told her, "Yeah, Mom. This whole college life—it just isn't for me."

We couldn't afford to buy me a plane ticket home—and I wasn't into flying again anyway—so my mom drove all the way to South Carolina to pick me up. And I swear the whole ride home, all I talked about was my dream. I told her, "I want to fight. I want to make it to the UFC. Just give me time. Give me a few years. I'll show you. I'll show everyone that I can do it."

The first thing I did when I got back to Uhrichsville was go hit Main Street Gym again. Working out in that woodshop felt right. It felt like home. But I was also a man now. I needed to start making money. So I got a job working in my Uncle Bob's concrete business. I'd wake up early every day, sometimes as early as four o'clock in the morning, to go run and sneak in a workout. Then I'd be out raking concrete all day on a construction site while daydreaming about fighting in the UFC. At night, after I punched out, I'd get in another workout before going to bed, waking up, and doing it all again.

That routine definitely worked for me for a while, and my dedication to training paid off. I found my stride. I found myself getting in better and better shape.

Only somehow, once I was firmly planted back in the 922, my dream started to slip further and further out of view.

SEVEN

ONCE I WAS BACK IN MY MOM'S HOUSE, IT DIDN'T take long before I fell in with some of my old crew and started partying again. I started drinking more than ever and found myself getting into street fights and bar fights again, too, almost every time I went out.

I didn't understand it at the time, but looking back I can see what was happening with me. After being in school my whole life, dedicating myself to wrestling and football and all the teamwork that comes with sports, suddenly I had no team. I felt like a big part of my life was missing, like I'd stepped into a dark tunnel, alone, and lost my way.

I wasn't the only one. One of my old childhood friends and sparring partners, my buddy A. J., got into some serious trouble when we were out one night. It was another one of those cases where I found myself inches away from getting seriously hurt or going to jail, while my buddy came even closer. That's when A. J. decided to do something about it. At nineteen years old, he decided to get baptized. He threw himself into the church the way we'd been throwing ourselves into partying. He changed his life, cold turkey. He was just sick and tired of all of the bull, so he started praying every day—and God changed him.

That inspired me. I admired what A. J. had done, and I wanted to change myself too. But the way I saw it, the cage was my church. Fighting was my way of honoring my talents and therefore honoring what God had given me. So I decided that what I needed to do was to throw myself back into my sport—but to do it a good safe distance from the 922. And while I was at it, I thought, maybe I should give college another try.

I had some old high school friends who were attending Notre Dame—not the football giant in Indiana, but Notre Dame College in South Euclid, Ohio, just east of the city of Cleveland. They said I could crash with them for a while if I wanted. I also found a gym in nearby Independence that was full of some really great MMA fighters. So I went up there to see if Strong Style MMA/ Old-School Boxing might have room to add me to their program. And while I was there, just to see what would happen, I applied for a wrestling scholarship at Notre Dame.

I got both.

This time, though, my attempt at going to college lasted only a week. I realized I'd made the same mistake all over again, trying to step into a world I didn't believe in and didn't have a true passion for. So I called home to tell my mom I was withdrawing from school. Again.

That left me only one path forward: I needed to make my dream come true. But the gym I joined wasn't willing to put me in a fight right away. They wanted to train me in their style of fighting first, to make sure I would be a positive influence on their winning record. I had to wait around until January of 2011 before that would happen. That left me in the Cleveland area struggling to pay rent—and to pay for my training at this new gym, which wasn't cheap—without any way to earn an honest living.

The only solution I could come up with was to move back home part time and drive back and forth to Cleveland while catching some construction work here and there and working for my Uncle Bob when he needed me. But Cleveland is almost two hours from Uhrichsville, and all that driving left me exhausted. Plus, I wound up spending weekends at home, which meant I was partying and getting into fights.

The whole thing felt wrong. This wasn't how it was supposed to go. Every time I went to work I felt like I was selling out. This wasn't my dream. This wasn't what I wanted to do. And no matter how hard I worked, I had no money left at the end of the month to show for it. So I started selling drugs again just to get by.

Before I knew it, I was almost twenty years old, and I was still living with my mom. The only fun I ever had was going out drinking and partying like I'd done when I was in high school. It didn't make any sense.

I won back-to-back fights in January and February of 2011. I TKO'd both fighters in the first round. But I only got into those fights by selling drugs. I had to sell drugs to get the money to pay for the blood work I needed to pass the drug tests to stay sanctioned. How messed up is that? Then I sold more drugs to cover the entry fees.

It became brutally clear to me that the only fighters who make any money in MMA were the guys who made it to the UFC. And that dream felt further away than ever.

One weekend that winter, I got drunk and wound up in a brawl. Two guys jumped me from behind, and I fought back until neither of them was standing. My brother was home visiting from his coal-mining job that weekend. And when he came to pick me up, he found me staggering on the side of the road.

"Cody? What the hell you doin', man? Get in!"

I climbed into his truck, and he asked, "What'd you do to your hand?"

I looked down at my blood-covered fist and noticed I had somebody's tooth stuck in between my knuckles.

"Damn!" I said. I picked it out and tossed it out the window.

The next morning I told Zach that none of this was working out for me. I didn't think I had what it took to make it. I was going nuts just trying to pay the bills. I asked him how he liked working in the coal mine, and he said he loved it. He was making good money. He'd bought himself a motorcycle. He was making rent. He even had a girlfriend.

That was the other thing that bothered me: I didn't really have time for a girlfriend with this life I was living. I partied with some girls and had flings with some of them, but it was never anything steady. Never anything real.

I thought maybe if I had a girlfriend things wouldn't seem so bad. But I didn't. And the way I saw it, things were just about as bad as they could get.

In a matter of just a few months, I had let my *vision* get clouded. I'd gotten so caught up in the day-to-day struggles of life that I'd lost sight of my dream.

I stopped thinking so much about making it to the UFC. I let that dream slip way back in my mind and decided I'd be better off making more "adult" decisions, including following in Zach's footsteps.

That Monday I enrolled in coal-mining school—a two-week intensive course. I passed. I got my certificate. I filled out some applications and got calls back from two different coal mines in Pennsylvania.

I had been drinking when I called Zach and told him what I was up to. I wanted his advice about which mine he thought would be best for me. But as soon as I asked the question he went silent.

"Zach, you there?" I asked.

"Yeah, bro. I'm right here. I just never expected to hear that my brother wants to work in a freaking coal mine."

"Well, yeah. I told you how broke I am. I told you how hard it's been. I just want things to be easier."

Zach went silent again.

"Yo!" I yelled into the phone. "You there?"

"Yeah. Cody. Look, man. I know it sounds like it would be easier to get a forty-hour-a-week job and just be set, you know? But these coal mines—I'm pulling down something like seventy hours a week. Six-day schedules. My whole life is work. You do that, and there won't be any time left for you to train."

"I don't care about that," I said. "I think I'm done with that."

"Done with what? Done with fighting? Are you kidding me?" Zach said. "Look, man, I work with a bunch of guys all day every day, and do you know what those guys talk about? Do you know what everyone who comes up to me wants to talk about?"

"What?"

"*You.* They want to know about you and how you're doing and when your next fight is."

"Why?" I asked.

"Because you're doin' it, man! Because you're driven. A lot of these guys dreamed of being fighters. They love fighting. But they don't have what it takes to make it. They aren't driven like you are. Hell, *I'm* not that driven.

That's why I dropped out. I wasn't gonna keep getting up at four or five in the morning to go run with you. Screw that! But you never stopped. I mean, do you ever just stop and grab a burger at freaking Wendy's or something?"

"No," I admitted.

"No, you don't! You eat right. You stick to your diet. I couldn't do that to save my life. None of these guys have that kind of discipline."

"Yeah, but—"

"Yeah, but nothin'. Do you know how many people actually do something great? Almost none. Almost none, man. To actually do something great—that's a rarity. If you quit now, and you have that burning in the back of your head—that doubt, that wondering if you quit too soon—that's going to eat you alive. You don't want that kind of regret in your life."

I didn't know what to say. I didn't know what to think. I had no idea that my brother cared that much about me being a fighter.

"Dude," Zach said, "you're the most talented athlete I've ever seen, all right? Don't quit now. Just don't. I know you haven't reached anywhere near your goal. So keep going. For me. For mom. For Uncle Bob. Mainly for you. You've gotta make it, man. There's no one who's got a shot like you do. Just keep going. Go until you absolutely can't go no more."

Zach's words ran round and round in my head. I couldn't believe he laid into me like that. Did he really mean it? Did he really think I was that talented?

I drove around town in the dark, listening to music, trying to wrap my head around it all. And the more I thought about it, the more I realized Zach was right. It was too early for me to give up. I couldn't even figure out why I'd wanted to give up. It didn't make sense. What the hell had happened to me?

A couple of days later, I sat my mom down at our old kitchen table—the same old brown table that had seen us through her multiple marriages and somehow survived without breaking under the weight of Zach and me crashing into it. My mom and Tim had split up by then, and she'd gotten remarried to a really nice guy named Mark. To everyone's surprise she'd gone and had another baby, too—my little sister, Hayley. Things just seemed real good with her lately. It was great having a little sister, and it was really great seeing my mom in what felt like a stable relationship.

I knew Mom wanted some of her new stability to rub off on me. She'd been happy when I went to coal-mining school and thrilled when I got those calls from two different mines. She was excited just thinking that I might settle down a little bit, keep out of trouble, and maybe make some steady money. But I told her, "Mom, I've decided I'm not going to take either of those jobs. I'm going to make it as a fighter."

"Cody—" she began in that exasperated way that moms do. But I wouldn't let her finish.

"I mean it this time," I said. "Give me five years. Give me 'til I'm twenty-five. If I haven't made it by then, I'll take whatever steady job I can get."

That's when my mom looked me in the eye and said, "Cody, you know I support you. Whatever you want to do—just do it with your whole heart. Do it 100 percent, okay? And if you say you can do it by the time you're twenty-five, then I'm gonna believe you—and I'm gonna hold you to it."

"Deal," I said. I gave her a hug, and the very next day I started commuting back and forth to Cleveland again. I set up another fight, this time on a big-time stage in what they billed as the "Super Bowl of MMA fighting in Ohio"—a NAAFS event called Fight Night in the Flats 7.

My gym put me up against a solid amateur fighter with a 5–1 record who was looking to go pro. Winning a fight like that could set me on a track to go pro myself, and that's exactly the kind of fight I needed if I was going to prove myself.

That fight wasn't easy. I struggled. There would be no KO this time; I'd have to endure all three rounds. But once again my striking abilities—thanks more to Uncle Bob's Numbers than anything I'd learned at my new gym—paid off. I won that fight in a unanimous decision.

I left Cleveland that night feeling on top of the world. I went home to spend a few quiet days recovering, knowing I was on my way.

I felt like I was finally back on course.

But the 922 wasn't done with me yet.

EIGHT

IT WAS A SATURDAY IN JUNE OF 2011. I WAS IN A good mood, relaxing with flip-flops on my feet, when a buddy of mine texted me from down at Tammie's Tavern. He needed a ride and was wondering if I could pick him up. I said, "Sure."

Tammie's Tavern sits on the outskirts of Uhrichsville, and just one look at the place pretty much tells you everything you need to know about the 922's reputation for trouble. The place sits on State Route 800 in a stand-alone building that looks a little bit like somebody's old, rundown house from the seventies. It's got light-blue siding, boarded-up windows on the second floor, and a concrete-block extension off the back. You might not know it was a bar at all if it wasn't for the neon Miller Lite sign in one of the two unboarded windows on one side, or the faded Tammie's Tavern sign up on the roof.

The sun was setting as I pulled into the gravel parking lot that day. I wasn't old enough to go into a bar. I wasn't even twenty yet, so not old enough to drink. But I managed to walk in with a group of other people, and in the chaos of the moment no one bothered to check my ID at the door. I wasn't looking for a drink anyway. I was just looking to pick up my buddy and give him a ride. But once I found him and a couple of other friends in the crowd, I decided to stay awhile.

Tammie's is about as divey as a dive-bar can get, but it's a fun place to hang out, and I enjoyed catching up with my friends while we checked out some of the local girls. It was crowded in there, though—maybe too crowded. I started to feel uneasy.

I'm not sure how the fight began. Maybe someone bumped someone else by accident and spilled his drink. Maybe somebody hit on somebody else's girl—that's how most fights tended to start in these parts. But once a couple of fists started flying inside, it felt like a scene from that Patrick Swayze movie *Roadhouse*. Everybody in the place jumped right into it.

"Take it outside!" someone yelled from behind the bar, and that's exactly what happened. The whole crowd pushed and shoved its way through the door out into the parking lot as the skies opened up and it started pouring.

I decided to head for my car. I was halfway there when some guy jumped me from behind. I pushed him off and yelled, "Yo! I'm not trying to fight." But this guy, an older guy, just wouldn't stop. He came at me swinging as more fights broke out all around us.

Something about the unexpected rain and the energy of that crowd amped everything up. It was out of control. I couldn't believe how many people were getting messed up out there all at once. I didn't want to be a part of it, but this guy took a swing at me and I had no choice. I cracked him with a jab right, then a left, and knocked him out cold.

I noticed one of my friends getting into it with some other kid as I yelled to my buddy who'd asked for a ride, "Let's go!" I walked backward to my car so I wouldn't get jumped again. My head was on swivel, trying to look everywhere at once so I wouldn't catch an unexpected blow from one of the other fights, but in the dark and the rain, it was hard to see. The next thing I knew, the kid who'd been fighting my buddy was up in my face running his mouth off.

I put my palms up and said, "Look, I'm not trying to fight," but the guy was relentless. I thought I recognized him—was pretty sure we'd gone to school together. I'd never had a problem with this kid before, and I didn't know what his problem was with me now, but for some reason it seemed personal to him.

"I've been to jail," he yelled. "I've been to prison!" As if that should make me respect him or be scared of him or something?

"Who cares, bro?" I said as I unlocked my truck and reached for the door handle. "It doesn't even matter."

What happened next struck me as weird. He threw his right hand out, kind of off to the side. I wasn't sure what he was doing.

Then I caught a glimpse of my buddy running toward us. He looked scared. "Watch out!" he yelled.

That's when the kid swung his fist down like he was pounding on a table and hit me hard in the chest. I felt a crack like a hammer to my sternum. *What the hell was that?* I thought. Suddenly my mind went into hyperdrive like it does when I'm in the octagon, reading every sign, every moment, every movement as it happens, trying to anticipate what's coming so I can find the opening I need to defend myself—or better yet, to strike and end the thing right there.

Somebody started up a car. Headlights lit up the parking lot. A beam of light glinted off the metal in this kid's hand, and I suddenly realized he was holding a knife. He had hit me with the blunt bottom edge of a switchblade, and he was about to hit me again—only this time he'd turned his fist over, and the blade was pointed right at me.

Before he had a chance to swing again, I leaned on my buddy and threw up a fast high head kick. *Smack!* The guy fell to the ground.

"He cut me, bro. He cut me!" my buddy said. "I tried to warn you."

My friend's bicep was gashed. It was bad. He jumped in the passenger seat of my truck and yelled, "Come on!"

I looked down at the ground at the guy with the knife and thought about cracking his skull open. But I didn't. He wasn't worth it. I took off, spinning my tires, spraying gravel and mud onto the dozens of bodies all splayed out behind us. The kid with the knife was still on the ground, and I'm pretty sure I saw some other guys kicking him while he was down. All I could think was, *He had it coming, man.*

We were back at my buddy's house in a matter of minutes and managed to get all the way inside before he said, "Oh sh-t, man." His eyes were wide. "He got you too."

I looked down to see where he was looking and saw blood. *My* blood. My left calf was gushing all over the floor. My adrenaline was pumping so hard that I didn't feel the pain until I saw the wound. His knife had sliced through my calf muscle just below the knee, cut it clean down to the bone. It must have happened when I kicked him—and now my calf muscle was just about falling off.

"You need to go to the hospital, man," my buddy said.

"Yeah," I said.

The trip to the hospital happened in a fog. I all but blacked out as a dark feeling sank into my chest—a recognition of just how close to the edge I'd come. That kid with all of his bragging talk about going to prison had literally just tried to kill me. It was nothing but a bar fight, a street brawl, the kind of thing I'd spent my life getting pulled into just for fun. Yet on that night, that kid had nearly ended me right then and there.

I came around as the doctors at the hospital stitched my calf back together. I stared at the white ceiling tiles and kept thinking: *If his fist had been turned in the other direction . . . if that blade had been facing the other way. . . .*

I'd gone and messed everything up. Again.

I started to wonder if maybe what happened in the parking lot of Tammie's was a sign. I closed my eyes as the last stitch went in and I prayed to God for answers. "Is this it? Is it over? Is this all my life is ever going to be?"

The pain in my leg was brutal, and I was tired of the roller coaster I'd been on. I was tired of everything.

I crossed my arms over my eyes and tried to block out the world. And when the doctors and nurses left the room, I begged God right out loud, "Tell me what You want from me! Tell me what to do. Because right now I feel like giving up on *everything*. Like, maybe I oughta just quit. Maybe I'm done trying. Maybe it's time to give in."

NINE

ONE DAY IN JULY, ZACH CALLED TO CHECK IN AND
see how I was doing, just as he'd done every few days since I got out of the
hospital. He could tell right away that I wasn't doing good. I was still in a lot
of pain and wallowing in self-pity.

He tried to cheer me up in his own way by telling me to stop being a wuss.
"Your leg will heal soon enough," he said, "and you'll be better than ever. So
stop your b-tching."

"Yeah, whatever." I wasn't in the mood for cheering up.

"By the way," he said, "did you hear about the Maple kid?"

"Who?"

"This kid in Dennison—Maddux Maple," Zach said. "Kid's five years
old, and he's got cancer. A bunch of people in town are trying to raise money
for the family and stuff. You should do something," he added. "Go visit the
kid, maybe give him some proceeds from your next fight. I bet you could
really help him out. Cheer him up if nothing else, since you're a big famous
fighter and all."

At that point I didn't even know if there would be a next fight. That one
trip to Tammie's had knocked me back to nothing. But I had time to kill, so
I went on Facebook while Zach was still on the phone and I found the page
dedicated to Maddux. I took one look at the photo of this little kid sitting in a
hospital bed, and I nearly lost it. The kid just looked so vulnerable.

When I got off the phone with Zach, I scrolled through all of the posts about Maddux. He looked about the same age as my little sister, maybe a little older. I don't know why it hit me so hard, but it did. Seeing that kid's picture made me think how terrible it would be if Hayley ever got sick. I couldn't get over how unfair it was for a kid that age to be stuck in a hospital bed fighting for his life instead of out having fun.

I sent a Facebook message to Maddux's father, Mic, telling him how sorry I was to hear about what his son was going through. I took Zach's suggestion and told Mic that I wanted to help, and I asked if I could meet his son.

I heard back from Mic that night. He thanked me but said a meeting wouldn't be possible. Maddux was just too sick to have any visitors.

I messaged him back and told him, "I understand." I didn't really understand, though. I couldn't possibly understand what that family was going through. But I mentioned again that I wanted to do something to help, and I asked Mic to let me know when Maddux was feeling better.

A couple of days later, as I changed the bandage on my leg, the pain was searing. It pissed me off that I wasn't healing quicker. Then Zach's voice—"Stop being a wuss"—popped into my irritated brain, and that made me think of Maddux. Would he ever get better? I went back to check my messages. Mic hadn't written back, so I sent him another note.

Mic responded that he was surprised to hear from me. He thanked me again, and he said he'd let me know as soon as Maddux was up for visitors. And then something really cool happened: Mic and I started messaging back and forth. Before long we had exchanged phone numbers and I was checking in regularly with both Mic and Stephani, his wife—just staying in touch, asking them how Maddux was doing, how they were doing.

I wanted to know everything. And they told me.

Mic and Stephani Maple spent their childhoods less than two miles from where I grew up, but somehow the world they described seemed a whole lot closer to "Dreamsville, USA."

Even though he's not a real tall guy, Mic had played basketball for as long as he can remember. And Steph played just about every sport she could—basketball, volleyball, softball, you name it. Softball was her thing, though. She pitched a no-hitter in high school and got local-famous for it.

"No-hitter" could serve as a pretty good description for both of their lives, too, because neither one of them can remember ever getting into a fistfight with anyone. Their families didn't watch fights for fun and didn't hang out in places where they wound up in bar fights or street brawls. They focused on pastimes that were a lot less brutal.

I didn't know a life like that could happen in the 922, and I didn't know Mic and Stephani when I was growing up. They're closer to my parents' age group than mine, and we obviously didn't run in the same circles.

Ask Steph to remember something from fifth grade, and she doesn't remember a fight or a probation officer. Instead, she talks about the time she went to watch her big brother play basketball at his friend's house. It was four blocks from where she lived, and she went home that night and told her mother, "I met the boy I'm going to marry!"

Her mother laughed. But Stephani didn't give up.

Mic was five years older. He was in high school. And he didn't want anything to do with Stephani. For years he would complain to his friend about how much she annoyed him. "She's like a little stalker. Why is she always hanging around?"

After Mic graduated from high school, when Stephani was a freshman, they ran into each other at a basketball game—and suddenly Steph didn't seem so annoying anymore. They went on their first date on New Year's Eve, 1997, and they've been together ever since.

By the time I met them, Mic and Stephani were both working in Stephani's family business, running group homes that cared for the mentally ill. Twenty years earlier, Stephani's aunt had seen that there was a need for more personalized service in the local mental health community, so she'd left her job as a nurse and created a group home. It grew, Steph's uncle took the reins, and soon there were a bunch of group homes in surrounding towns. Mic and Steph were in their twenties and married when they stepped in as a team to help manage those homes. Their work definitely kept them both running, but somehow they managed to build a really nice life for themselves.

They settled just a few blocks from the Dennison Railroad Depot Museum—right up the street from the Dennison Yard, an Italian restaurant that's one of my all-time favorite places to eat anywhere. (There's something really cool and homey about that spot.) And even though their house was smack dab in the heart of the 922, the Maples tried to make the most of life in every way they could.

Back in the spring of 2011, everything was going well for this family. Mic and Stephani had two young kids—Maddux, who was about to turn five, and his little sister Makyah (pronounced "Ma-KAI-ah"), then three—plus two little dogs. And after battling an illness, Stephani's mother had recently moved in with them, too, making for one big, happy family with the bonus of a built-in grandma babysitter.

One day that June, just as Maddux was getting ready to graduate from preschool, he complained to Steph that his heart hurt. "Your heart?" she asked, just a little alarmed. Steph's admittedly a bit of a worrier. She didn't want to overreact, but Maddux wasn't the kind of kid who ever complained. So she brought him over to see her sister Michelle, who is a nurse. She checked him out and noted that he didn't have a fever and wasn't short of breath. And since he'd stopped complaining by the time she saw him, Michelle said, "Steph, he's fine."

Stephani wasn't totally convinced. He still seemed a little "off" to her. A few days later, heading into Saturday night—maybe the exact same Saturday when I was getting ready to go pick up my buddy at Tammie's Tavern—Mic and Steph managed to get off work at the same time. Since that rarely happened, they decided to make the most of it and have a family night out. They took the kids up to the mall in Canton. They went out to eat, spent some time at the mall's Build-a-Bear Workshop, and took in a movie the kids had been dying to see. Then, on Sunday, they all went and celebrated a cousin's birthday at a big family party.

As Steph recalls it, when her head hit the pillow on Sunday night she couldn't stop smiling. She turned and said to her husband, "That was pretty much the perfect family weekend."

"Yeah," Mic agreed. "It's been too long. We need to do that more often."

Sometime in the middle of Sunday night, Maddux crawled into Mic and Steph's bed feeling sick, and at two o'clock that Monday morning he woke up moaning in agonizing pain.

"What is it?" Steph asked.

"My stomach," Maddux cried. "My stomach!"

Steph checked his temperature. He was running a slight fever. She tried to calm him down, but she couldn't. Maddux was a sweet kid and anything but a complainer, so Steph knew something was really wrong. It didn't seem serious enough to warrant a trip to the emergency room, but she took Maddux to the pediatrician first thing in the morning.

The doctor quickly ruled out any sort of food-borne illness. He pressed on Maddux's stomach and pelvis and worried that the appendix might be inflamed. So he sent Maddux over to the local hospital for a CT scan.

That's when something really strange happened. The doctors at the hospital said they couldn't find Maddux's appendix on the scan. That could mean only one thing, they said: the appendix must have ruptured. It was a life-threatening situation. Maddux needed surgery. Now.

They rushed Maddux into an ambulance headed for Akron Children's Hospital. Steph called Mic and her mom and broke down on the phone trying to explain what was happening. Mic dropped everything and drove to Akron so fast that he actually beat the ambulance. Steph's mom showed up moments later, and they both did their best to comfort Stephani while a surgeon examined Maddux once more.

Maddux had been a trooper through the whole ordeal, she told them. He hadn't cried or anything. He just wanted to feel better, and he didn't seem to know why his mom was so upset.

The confusing part was when the surgeon at Akron Children's decided not to operate. "They said at the other hospital that his appendix has ruptured," Stephani argued. "You need to get in there right now!"

"I read their report," the surgeon replied, "but it's not adding up. You see, when I press here," he said, pushing gently on Maddux's abdomen, "there should be more acute pain. But there isn't. The pain is coming and going. That doesn't indicate the appendix. If it had ruptured, his fever would likely be much higher too. It just doesn't make sense. I want to keep him overnight and run some more tests."

The doctors never received an answer about why the appendix hadn't shown up in the initial scans, but they were happy that it hadn't actually ruptured. Maddux was spared from the knife that Monday afternoon.

The next morning the hospital ran some blood work, and the labs came back with troubling results. Maddux's white-blood-cell count was through the roof. Normal is between 10 and 13. His was 47.3. The resident told Mic and Steph that this could indicate an infection or any of a few other things.

Including leukemia.

Just the mention of that word, even if it was a remote possibility, meant Maddux wouldn't be going home anytime soon. There would be more tests. And even though nothing was confirmed in that moment, when the doctor walked out of the room, Steph broke down crying. She knew. As a mom and as someone who works in and around the medical field, she says she just knew.

Mic got kinda mad at her response. "Why do you go there?" he asked her. "Why do you go to the very worst thing?"

But Steph insisted. Their son, their sweet little five-year-old boy, had cancer.

When they told me about it, I felt like I was right there with them. I can't explain it, but I felt like I'd known Mic and Stephani my whole life. They were strangers to me, yet I cared about what they had been through the same way I would have cared if it was happening to someone in my own family.

I got chills when Stephani said the word *cancer*. Hearing it from her own voice, I understood just how devastating it must have been for her to sit in that doctor's office and hear those words. I imagined she was talking about Hayley or my mom or Zach.

This family had somehow managed to dodge all the fights and trouble the 922 had to offer. They had no warning that they were about to get thrown into the fight of their lives.

TEN

MIC AND STEPHANI HAD TAKEN MADDUX TO SEE his pediatrician on Monday morning. By Tuesday afternoon, they were sitting down with Dr. Jeffrey Hord, one of the top oncologists at Akron Children's Hospital, who confirmed any parent's worst nightmare.

Dr. Hord told them he was moving Maddux up to the fifth floor. The cancer floor.

By the time Maddux's room was ready, just about his whole extended family had gathered in the waiting rooms. His grandparents and aunts and uncles and cousins took turns rotating into Maddux's room to lend their support.

Mic and Stephani never left their son's side.

Dr. Hord spent a good forty-five minutes with them that day explaining options, talking through treatment possibilities, and laying out what sounded like an impossibly long road ahead, no matter how they chose to move forward. Finally, after the nurses had administered some pain meds and Maddux was sound asleep, Mic and Stephani stepped out of the room, away from everyone, and walked down a little hallway all by themselves. They found a quiet spot, sat down, and collapsed into each other's arms.

Neither one of them can remember exactly how long they sat there, letting the weight of that news sink in. If they could have stayed right there, just the two of them, and hidden away from it all, they probably would have. But their cocoon was broken when Dr. Hord walked over and put his hands on their shoulders.

"You can do this," he said to them.

They weren't sure they could. Who could ever be sure of such a thing?

"We've scheduled a bone-marrow biopsy for tomorrow morning, first thing. After that we'll know exactly what we're dealing with and can treat it appropriately. So we'll hope for the best. And just know—I mean it—you guys can do this. Maddux can do this. I can already tell he's a fighter."

That night, Steph and Mic prayed for their son. They prayed for God's help. They prayed that somehow they would wake up and this whole thing would just be a dream. A nightmare, sure, but at least something that wasn't real.

They barely slept. In the morning the doctors asked if they would like to be in the room with Maddux for the marrow biopsy. Steph, of course, said yes.

Akron is a teaching hospital, so no sooner had they entered the room than it was flooded with young doctors in training. Everyone assured Steph and Mic that Maddux was young enough that he wouldn't remember this procedure at all, even though he would be awake and the marrow would be harvested under a local anesthetic. But the procedure would probably be difficult for *them* to watch, something they would likely never forget.

"That's okay," Steph and Mic said. They wanted to be there.

Then the tool came out. The bone-marrow aspiration needle that would soon enter their son's body looked like a long drill bit capped on one end by a plastic handle. It was a couple inches long, shiny, and horrifying. Steph said it looked like the sort of a tool somebody might use to screw in a football cleat or a track spike. She took one look at it and felt sick to her stomach.

Mic held her hand and sent up a silent prayer: *God, I hope You're here with us. Please make Maddux okay. Please get us through this.*

Maddux held up fine through the small incision. He didn't feel a thing. But when they put that big syringe down into Maddux's leg and the doctor cranked the handle clockwise to start drilling into the bone, Maddux screamed. He screamed bloody murder. Stephani couldn't take it. She nearly threw up.

They twisted the handle again. Maddux screamed even louder. And Stephani left her husband alone to hold Maddux's hand as she ran from the room, bawling, into the arms of her mother.

"I can't do this. I can't do this. I can't take it," she cried. She could still hear her little boy screaming through the closed door.

"You *can* do this," her mother insisted, "and you will. What choice do you have?"

Her mother's voice steadied her—until Maddux screamed again.

"God!" Steph cried out. "Please make it stop!"

Seconds later, God answered her prayer, at least for the short term. Her son stopped screaming. The procedure was over. And it had gone well. The doctors had gotten what they needed.

By noon, they confirmed with 100-percent certainty that Maddux did, in fact, have leukemia. By five o'clock that afternoon, they knew it was something called acute lymphoblastic leukemia, or ALL. According to Dr. Hord, that was a very good thing. It was the best they could hope for. ALL was the most treatable form of leukemia in children.

Dr. Hord explained it all to Maddux in a way a five-year-old could understand. He told him he had bad guys in his blood and that the doctors needed to get in there and fight the bad guys with medicine. They would hook him up to some advanced machines to flush his blood out and give him some fresh blood, and then the chemotherapy would put good guys into his blood to knock any leftover bad guys out.

Dr. Hord then asked the family if they wanted to start treatment right away or to wait. Steph and Mic looked at each other like, *What is there to think about? Of course we want to start!*

The staff walked them through all sorts of scenarios before they would let them sign off on it, though. They told them that because of the treatment, there could be long-term side effects. Maddux might not be able to have kids when he got older, and the treatment might put him at a higher risk for developing other types of cancer in his twenties. The staff told them that some parents think those side effects are enough to warrant holding off or maybe trying something else first. But Stephani was thinking, *We're already at one of the best hospitals in the country. There's no use wasting time on a second opinion. There's no sense in holding off. If we don't try this, then he's not going to make it to his twenties.*

They scheduled surgery for Thursday morning to install a port in Maddux's chest.

Maddux hadn't shed a tear over any of the tests or procedures—other than the bone-marrow biopsy. But later that night, when the three of them lay together in Maddux's hospital bed, the little fighter finally broke down. Mic told me that all three of them started crying in that bed. They held each other and cried for a solid hour, until finally the crying just stopped and Maddux fell fast asleep.

The next morning he had his port installed, and that afternoon he sat through his first dose of chemo.

Steph and Mic couldn't get over it. This whole thing had come out of nowhere and jumped them from behind. They never saw it coming. In just a few days, their lives had been completely overturned.

Worry and prayer replaced sleep. They worried, not just about Maddux, but about everything that now seemed on hold. How would they ever be able to go back to work? How would they pay for all of this, even with insurance? Neither of them had ever prayed so hard in their lives, they told me. They thanked God that Stephani's mom had moved in when she did, but they couldn't help but wonder how this would all affect Makyah, whom they hadn't seen in four days.

Four days. That's all it had been. Four days to go from the perfect family weekend to their son starting chemotherapy for leukemia.

Four days.

Over the course of the next four weeks, Mic and Stephani watched their son transform into someone almost unrecognizable. Maddux had always been a happy-go-lucky kid who always had a smile on his face. He was naturally sweet and always kind. He helped out around the house. He enjoyed music and watching shows like *Yo Gabba Gabba!*, *The Fairly OddParents*, and *Jake and the Never Land Pirates* on TV. He loved his little sister and his teachers and friends at preschool, and they loved him back. But Dr. Hord warned Mic and Stephani that the physical changes brought on by the chemo might be hard to watch, and he said the way Maddux's personality would change once they started him on a high dose of steroids might make it even harder.

Despite the warnings, the changes in Maddux shocked them all. He dropped weight fast and was down to skin and bones, but the steroids caused his cheeks to puff out like a chipmunk. Most of his hair fell out.

Then there was the night when they were all at home in front of the TV and Maddux asked his mom for some pizza rolls. Everybody heard him say it—Mic, Stephani's mom, even Makyah. Steph said, "Sure," and went to the kitchen. She was happy that he still had an appetite. When she returned and handed him his plate full of pizza rolls, Maddux got mad—really mad. He got red in the face and yelled, "I said I wanted chicken nuggets!"

Stephani was shocked. Maddux had never raised his voice to her. Ever. She looked around the room. The whole family was frozen.

Steph held it together. "Okay," she said. She took the pizza rolls back into the kitchen, and when she was out of her son's sight, she lost it. Tears flooded down her cheeks. The chemo and steroids were clearly wreaking havoc on his body and his mind. But thankfully, Maddux's moodiness and irritability didn't last long.

One day as Stephani drove him home from Akron Children's, Maddux said, "Mom, I'm going to get sick." She wasn't prepared for that, and she couldn't pull over in traffic, so like some kind of supermom she scanned the car for something that might be capable of catching a kid's puke. She spotted a McDonald's bag on the floor, reached down, grabbed it, and handed it back to Maddux in two seconds flat.

She was just in time. He threw up into the bag and didn't spill a drop. "I'm done," he said in a chipper voice, as if it was no big deal.

That was the easygoing Maddux they were used to. Steph was so glad that he didn't seem upset about puking. "Good job gettin' it all in the bag!" she told him. Seconds later, the bottom of that thin paper bag broke through, and hot vomit fell all over Maddux's legs, his shoes, his car seat, the backseat, and the car's carpeted floor.

From that day forward, the family kept a designated puke bucket in every vehicle and in every room in the house. Maddux didn't throw up all that often, but when he did, it came on suddenly, and those buckets saved them a lot of cleanup.

The thing that upset Mic and Steph most was how tired Maddux was. Sometimes in the middle of the day he'd be up for twenty minutes, get exhausted, and then go to sleep for four hours. There were days when he just never left his bed. Steph would crawl right in there and hold him for as long as she could. Even when he was up and playful, he was lethargic. Mic said it reminded him of being around a kid with the flu or pneumonia, only it never went away.

One good thing about the modern world—we can connect with people through social media and develop friendships before we ever meet someone in real life. That's what happened with me and the Maple family. By exchanging messages and photos and sharing our stories, I got to know them and they got to know me, all in the span of a few weeks.

Mic and Stephani passed along my messages to Maddux and showed him photos of me in the ring. They told him I was a fighter who'd grown up right there in their hometown, and they told me Maddux thought that was "really cool." The kid seemed to like the fact that this local fighter was pulling for him, and I was glad I could put a smile on his face.

Mic and Steph poked a little fun at me one time, saying they knew the Garbrandt name—and knew it meant trouble. I promised them I was less trouble than my family's reputation might let on. "I've never been arrested or anything like that," I said, which was true. And they seemed to get a kick out of the fact that a Garbrandt kid was sincere in wanting to help their son.

I decided I wanted to give Maddux something that would inspire him to keep fighting. Maybe a pair of boxing gloves. I wasn't sure what I was going to do yet.

Maybe it was just a coincidence, but as all of this was going on, I started to feel a little better myself. My leg finally turned a corner to where I got enough strength back to get out on the mats and start training again. I got up off my butt and I regained some focus.

I realized I wasn't ready to give up on my dreams.

ELEVEN

ABOUT A MONTH AFTER WE'D MADE OUR FIRST
contact, Mic sent me a message saying Maddux wasn't doing well.

The treatment in the first thirty days had been so intense that it rocked
the poor kid's body. Mic and Steph made a habit of staying close, sometimes
holding Maddux's arm to steady him when he walked. On this day his legs
had been weak and his balance was not so good. Mic went with him into the
bathroom to help him brush his teeth.

When Maddux turned to grab a hand towel, his legs gave out and he collapsed. It happened in an instant. Mic tried to stop his son's fall, but he just
couldn't reach him in time. Maddux slammed his head onto the hard tile floor
with a whack that Mic said he would never forget.

They rushed to the hospital. Maddux was okay, but he would need a
wheelchair until he regained some strength. He kind of liked the idea of getting pushed around by his parents, but Mic felt awful. He texted me saying
he felt like a failed father. I texted back that it wasn't his fault, that sometimes
things just happen. I told him the story about the concussion I'd suffered
when I was that age at the hands of my brother and said I had recovered just
fine. That didn't seem to help much. Stephani tried to reassure Mic, too, but
I could tell he was beating himself up over it.

I felt bad for the guy. I really didn't know what to do or say, but it meant
something that he had reached out to me. I admired him a lot. This guy I
hadn't even met in person was exactly the kind of father I wanted to be to my

own kids someday. He was clearly a rock to his family. And it felt good to be there for him in any small way I could.

That was the thing I kept thinking about. The Maples were good people living a good life, and having that contact with them lit a fire in me. I wanted to do better. I needed to live better. All my running around, getting into bar fights, getting stabbed—what was I doing?

I was a fighter. I was a great fighter. I'd been messing around with this back-and-forth of training hard and then getting into trouble for way too long. I'd wasted too much time trying to live up to other people's expectations, too, and wasted too much energy doing things that didn't help me—or help anyone else for that matter.

It's amazing how caring about somebody else, even somebody you only know from a distance, can change your focus in life. I found myself thinking about Maddux and his family instead of worrying about my own sh-t all the time.

I wasn't sure what I was going to do in response or how I was going to help, but I was certain that I wanted to. I knew I wanted to be there for Mic, for Steph, and for Maddux.

When back-to-school time came around for Maddux, he was too sick to go. So the school had to send over a tutor, and the tutor who stepped up just happened to be the principal of Claymont Elementary, Mr. Page.

Mr. Page was a super nice guy. Mic and Steph couldn't believe their good luck, and none of their friends could believe that a respected school principal would be willing to step out of his administrative shoes to go tutor a kid. But that was the kind of support Maddux seemed to pull from all over our little twin cities.

I heard stories from Mic and Stephani about how Mr. Page would be sitting there with Maddux at the kitchen table, reviewing the alphabet or something, when all of a sudden Maddux would vomit all over the place. Sometimes it came on too quickly to get the buckets, even when they were in the very same room. By that point, though, his parents were so used to it they'd just hop into action, grabbing wipes and bags and paper towels to clean up the mess. But it had to be awkward for poor Mr. Page. He would always tell Maddux he could come back and start again the next day, but according to Mic, Maddux never wanted his tutor to leave. "No, no, we can keep going," he would say.

Maddux's unwavering positive attitude blew his parents away.

As summer turned into fall, Maddux's health kept declining. He developed a sinus infection that got so bad the doctors recommended surgery. But once they got to the hospital for his presurgical exam, the doctors found something that shocked everyone. Maddux had developed mouth sores from the chemotherapy pills he'd been taking. He had one sore on the roof of his mouth that was like a crater—the size of a fifty-cent piece and nearly half an inch deep. When they scoped it out a little more, they saw that Maddux had similar sores all the way down his esophagus.

He'd never told his parents about them. In fact, he had never complained. Not once.

With all of those sores, there was no way they could go ahead with the surgery, so the doctors kept Maddux in the hospital to try to get him healed up. That's when things really started to go downhill. The little man kept getting infection after infection. Soon he wasn't allowed to eat. He had to fast for two and a half weeks.

Steph fasted right along with him, just so he wouldn't have to go through it alone. "If he can't eat, I can't eat—you know what I mean?" Stephani told me.

That's some hardcore loyalty right there.

Steph stayed there with Maddux day after day, night after night, while his pulse-ox levels (the oxygen in his blood) kept dropping and the sinus infection turned into a stomach infection, then a bowel infection. October stretched into November, and Maddux never left the hospital. Doctors could not figure out why he wasn't getting better. They put IVs into both of his little arms in addition to the port that they'd already installed in his chest, and they kept giving him all sorts of medications through all three of those holes in his body.

None of it helped.

Even after a month, Steph refused to leave Maddux's side.

Anyone who came into his room had to suit up and wear a mask and gloves, but Steph refused to hold her son with gloves on. She told me, "I got into a little argument with the nurse because she was like, 'You need to have a gown and stuff.' And I said, 'Ma'am, I have been with him since the day we came in here, and the last thing I'm going to do is sit here and hold my baby with freaking gloves and a mask on.' Because I kept thinking, *What if this is the last time I get to hold my baby?*"

Steph was so emotional at that point. Mic tried everything he could think of to comfort her. But Maddux? Maddux didn't complain. He didn't complain about anything, even the fasting. He took it all like a champ.

Meanwhile, I still hadn't figured out how I was going to help this kid and his family. I didn't have any money. I didn't have anything to offer them except a supportive text or a phone call. And as his condition grew worse, I felt like I'd been left standing on the sidelines while the game ticked away.

On November 16, 2011—which just happened to be Mic's birthday—one of the doctors pulled Mic and Steph aside and told them things were not looking good for their son. He had developed double-lung pneumonia, and despite every medication and effort they'd made, it wasn't clearing.

"To be perfectly frank," the doctor said, "we aren't sure what else we can do for him."

I can hardly begin to imagine how those words must have hit both Steph and Mic. I hadn't even met Maddux in person, and I was absolutely terrified that we were going to lose him. I checked my phone almost obsessively, picking it up every few minutes, even in the middle of workouts, just hoping and praying that I'd get some good news from Mic. Any news from Mic.

I went back on Facebook and looked at the very first photo of Maddux—the shot of that innocent kid sitting in a hospital bed. The photo that for some reason had caught me so off guard and inspired me to reach out to Mic in the first place. I clicked on the picture and blew it up so I could look into Maddux's big blue eyes. Did he know, even then, that he was in a fight for his life? Did he have any idea just how hard this was going to be? I wondered where he found that strength of his. And now that I was looking a little closer, that's definitely what I saw in that little man's eyes: strength.

I went to bed that night feeling totally helpless. I pictured those eyes that I'd only seen in photos, and I prayed to God that Maddux would be okay. I fell asleep, and at some point during the night I woke up with a vision of that little boy standing next to me. We were in a stadium full of people. He was walking beside me. He was strong. The crowd was cheering.

The next morning, I knew clearly what I wanted to do for Maddux. What I needed to do.

I called Mic and Stephani and told them I was going to donate all of the proceeds from my next fight to their son. They were taken aback and said that was way too generous, but I knew it was the least that I could do.

In the time we'd spent getting to know each other, my calf muscle had healed up pretty well. I'd managed to stay out of trouble for a few months too. And I'd managed to find what felt like a whole new rhythm and drive in my training.

I felt like I was finally ready to fight.

We set a date: on February 18, 2012, I'd go three rounds with Jerrell Hodge at an NAAFS event in Cleveland called Caged Vengeance 10.

I knew that Mic and Steph were living hour by hour in that hospital and that February seemed a long way off. But I told them that my greatest hope in the world was that Maddux would be there for that fight.

"I not only want him to be there," I said, "but I want him to walk me out to the octagon. I want him to know what it feels like for a whole stadium full of people to cheer him on."

"Wow," Mic said. "That would be incredible."

I told them that I'd hype up that fight as much as I could and that if we worked together we could get the whole 922 to buy tickets and come up to Cleveland. That way we could raise a lot of money. Maybe we could sell T-shirts and get the whole audience wearing them to show Maddux how much this whole community cared about him.

I could almost hear the wheels turning in Stephani's head while we were on the phone. She said her sister could help get T-shirts printed up.

Mic and Steph kept saying how grateful they were to me for wanting to help out, even though I hadn't done anything but share the idea at that point.

I'm sure they must've had doubts about whether it would all come together. But I didn't. I knew that the vision I'd had was real. I just hoped they could see it too.

Making that phone call and lining up that fight gave me something to look forward to—the first thing I'd looked forward to in almost a year. But the best part was that it wasn't for me. This wasn't just another fight. It wasn't even just a big fight, one that had the potential to launch me into the pros. This felt like something more.

I hoped I'd also given Mic and Stephani something to look forward to, something that would get their heads out of that hospital and the constant worry and stress. I hoped I had given them something new to talk about and plan for and share with their son.

They did share that news with him, right after we got off the phone, and they texted me back saying Maddux's face had lit up. He'd told them he couldn't wait to see me fight. I wasn't sure if they'd mention the part about walking out with me or not, but that was okay. I looked forward to asking him in person myself, hopefully sometime soon.

Having something positive to look forward to sure makes a difference in life. I just hoped it would be enough to make some sort of a difference to Maddux.

A couple of days before Thanksgiving, Maddux's health finally took another turn—this time for the better. On Thanksgiving Day he was doing so well that his doctors let his parents take him out for the holiday. They discharged him at noon, and without telling a soul, Mic and Stephani drove straight to Steph's aunt's house and surprised the whole family just as they sat down for turkey dinner.

Maddux was the center of love and attention for that whole day. He was even able to sleep in his bed that night and the next. It looked like I might finally get a chance to meet him that very weekend. But on Saturday he started to feel sick again and was readmitted to the hospital.

The emotional roller coaster of it all was so exhausting for Mic and Steph, I couldn't understand how they were still standing. Let alone that kid, who once again settled into a hospital room without complaint and spent all his time telling the nurses about how much fun he'd had at Thanksgiving.

It wasn't until mid-December that I finally got a text message saying, "Maddux doing better."

I called Mic back, and he told me that Maddux had managed to fight through everything—the mouth sores, the infections, the pneumonia, all of it. The doctors at Akron Children's were stunned. The kid went through another round of surgeries and spinals and came out the other side smiling.

"Dr. Hord told Maddux he has seventeen-year-olds in there who cry when they get spinals," Mic told me. "He said Maddux was the toughest kid in this whole place!"

Maddux seemed happy as could be just to sit in that hospital and wait it out while he and his parents wore out their copies of his favorite board games, Trouble and Guess Who? As we kept in touch and put all the plans together for the big fight, Maddux kept on getting better.

Finally, just a couple of days before Christmas, Maddux was able to go home. And this time the doctors said they didn't expect he'd need to come back anytime soon. All he had to do was take it easy, keep away from crowds and strangers for a while, and continue to take his medicine.

As we all looked ahead to the end of a very long 2011 and the start of a brand-new year, I'm pretty sure that Steph and Mic started to experience the same sort of thing I was feeling. Something none of us had felt a whole lot of since Maddux went back into that hospital in early October. Something I hadn't felt since I'd come so close to giving up on my fighting career altogether before I first heard Maddux Maple's name.

That thing we all felt? It's a feeling of knowing that your prayers have been heard. Maybe they haven't all been answered yet. But they've been heard.

There's a word for that feeling.

It's called *hope*.

TWELVE

IN JANUARY—SEVEN LONG MONTHS SINCE I'D
first reached out to Mic on Facebook—I finally got the call I'd been waiting
for. Maddux was not only doing better, but his immune system had grown
stronger. His doctor said it was safe for Maddux to have visitors—and Mic and
Stephani wondered if I still wanted to come over.

"Hell, yes!" I said.

I'd picked up a pair of white kid-sized boxing gloves to give to Maddux
a few months earlier, so I found them, signed them, threw them in my truck,
and hauled it down to the Maples' house as fast as I could.

It was January 22, 2012, and after all that time spent getting to know the
family through Facebook, phone calls, and texts, I felt like I was on my way
to see some long-lost friends. I was finally about to look Maddux Maple in the
eyes—not in some picture, but in real life.

As I pulled into the driveway, I couldn't help but notice that the Maples'
house was a perfect reflection of who they seemed to be as a family. The yard
was a little kid's paradise, with an above-ground pool and a trampoline and a
deck with plenty of room for hanging out with family and friends. It was so
well kept it almost looked like it had gotten picked up from some nicer town
somewhere and plopped down on this little corner lot in Dennison.

There was a chain-link fence around the yard, too, which was sort of an
unusual sight in that part of town. Most of the yards just bumped right up
against each other. It was almost as if that fence was there to keep the troubled

parts of the 922 out and keep the family safe inside. I liked that. These were people who put family first and made the most of what they had.

I was nervous as I walked up to the door, though. It was weird. I didn't get nervous climbing into a ring to face an opponent who wanted to beat the crap out of me, but this walkup gave me butterflies in my stomach. I guess I'd just been waiting for that moment for so long that I'd turned it into a really big deal in my head. I still can't explain why connecting with Maddux and his parents felt so important to me, but it did.

I shouldn't have worried, though. As soon as Steph and Mic opened that door and I saw them standing there side by side, all of my nerves went away. They were both smiling, and without even thinking about it we gave each other hugs.

"Maddux can't wait to meet you," Steph said as they led me into the living room. And there he was, sitting on the couch—the boy from the pictures. The wide-eyed kid who'd inspired me from afar.

"Hey, buddy," I said.

Maddux looked at me with a shy smile and said, "Hi." And it suddenly hit me just how much this kid's whole world had been turned upside down. His hair was gone. All of it. *Gone.* I'd seen that in pictures, but it was different in person. It knocked me out to imagine what that must've felt like for him—to no longer look like any of the other kids at school or even his own sister or mom and dad. To physically look so different. To look like someone other people might assume was dying.

I handed him the boxing gloves, and he smiled and tried them on. I pointed out where I'd signed them for him, and he smiled and nodded.

"I got you these gloves 'cause I know you're a fighter," I said. "I know you've been fighting hard every day."

Maddux didn't say anything. He just kept looking at the gloves and looking at me. He looked like a little warrior. He'd clearly been beaten down. He'd been through battle. He was scarred from it. But that boy knew he wasn't going anywhere. One look in his eyes, and there was no question.

I spent the next hour talking about all sorts of things with Mic and Steph. They wanted to know about my training and my upcoming fight. We talked about the logistics of selling tickets and T-shirts. They asked a little bit about my dad and my mom and how my brother was doing. I asked them what the latest news was from Maddux's doctors, and they wound up telling me a whole bunch of other stories about how tough Maddux had been in the hospital.

Maddux didn't say one word the entire time.

He didn't have to.

That kid and I connected just by looking at each other.

I didn't want to take up too much of their time, and I got the sense that Maddux was getting tired, so I finally looked right at him and said, "Look, if your parents will let you, and if you're up for it, I'd like you to walk me out to my next fight."

Maddux looked at his parents. I'm not sure he knew what I was talking about.

"What do you think, Maddux?" Mic said. "Would you like to walk Cody out to one of his fights?"

Maddux nodded.

"I don't know that he'll be ready by February," Steph said.

"Well, that's okay," I said. "I'll be ready whenever you are. I've got a lot of fights in front of me. I'm planning on making it to the UFC, and I know you're going to beat this. So whenever you're ready, you're gonna walk me out to the octagon, all right? You and me, bro—we're in this together."

Maddux nodded and gave me that shy smile again. I held a fist out to him, and he rock-pounded it.

"All right, kiddo. Stay strong," I said, moving into a fighting stance and smiling at him.

Maddux nodded again and gave me one last look with those warrior eyes. Then we said our good-byes and I left.

Mic called me the next day and apologized for how quiet Maddux had been. "As soon as you left, he got all excited and talkative. He was so happy to meet you, and he loved the gloves. I think he was just a little scared of all the tattoos or something. He didn't know what to make of you."

"That's okay," I said with a laugh. "I get it. He's five!"

I was glad Mic called. But deep down, I knew that Maddux and I had connected. The moment I looked at him, I loved him like a brother. You can see a lot in someone's eyes if you really look. I had pretty much mastered reading my opponents in fights, and I could tell that Maddux and I were kindred spirits. As different as we were, not just in age but in upbringing and family backgrounds, we were both fighters from the 922. Only Maddux wasn't fighting with his fists. He wasn't fighting his neighbors or fighting for dominance or fighting over some girl or because of some insult. He wasn't fighting what felt like an inescapable fate passed down from his father and grandfather.

Maddux was fighting for his *life*.

If Maddux, this little kid, this child who was so new to life, could find the strength to do battle with cancer, then I most certainly could find the strength to fight off the demons that kept popping up in my life.

I meant what I had said to him too. We were in this together.

I left Maddux's house feeling closer than ever to my faith and ready to pray. Not just sometimes. Not just occasionally. Just like my buddy A. J., I realized it was time for me to start praying every day.

Before I heard the name Maddux Maple, I was one decision away from ruining my life. I was one bad decision from throwing it all away. But as soon as I locked my eyes with his, I realized that it was in my power—through prayer and inspiration and hard work—to change my circumstances if I wanted.

Seeing Maddux in person reminded me just how precious life is and that anyone's life could be gone in an instant. So starting the very next morning, as soon as my feet hit the ground, I told God, "Thank You for another day." I've started every day since being thankful, too, and praying to God to please take care of me and my whole family.

That doesn't mean that I'm happy every day or that there aren't days when I wake up angry at the world. I have those days, of course. We all do. But even on those days I start by getting up and saying, "Thank You. Thank You for another day and for the air in my lungs. Now let's go tackle this day and get better and better."

Maddux gave me that inspiration.

THIRTEEN

THE LIGHTS WENT DOWN. THE MUSIC WENT UP. The crowd cheered. It was time.

The first thing I noticed as I started my walkout were the shirts. Orange shirts. Everywhere. A huge portion of the crowd in that Cleveland arena had purchased one of the "Madd for Maddux" shirts that Mic and Stephani sold to raise funds for their son. Mic's sister had them printed up from a guy who sold them the shirts for five bucks each. They sold them for ten, which meant they made a pretty good chunk of change.

But something else struck me about all of those orange shirts: they matched the shirt I was wearing. All of those people were in solidarity with me. They were on my side, fighting for Maddux. There was power in that.

I put "Madd for Maddux" on my fight shorts, too—right alongside the number 922.

But Maddux himself wasn't beside me. He wasn't there for the walkout. His immune system was still too weak to handle such a large crowd, so he stayed home. But his parents and a whole bunch of his friends, family, neighbors, and supporters from all over were there in that crowd, and I felt the energy of every one of them.

These were more than fans. They weren't there just to root for me. They were there for Maddux, and that made this fight all the more important.

In the lead-up to the match, I handed Mic and Stephani a stack of cash from all the tickets I'd sold. They tried to refuse it. They said I'd done enough already. But I insisted. That wasn't my money. It hadn't been my money since the moment I offered it up. It was all for them. For Maddux. They could donate it to cancer research if they wanted or use it to pay bills or take Maddux on a trip somewhere—whatever they wanted.

I never could have imagined how good it felt to hand over that money. I never could have imagined it could feel so profitable to go into a fight like that knowing I wouldn't be walking away with that stack of cash myself. But it did. I felt rich just knowing I was doing something right, something good, something that mattered.

Just about everything else about that fight felt wrong, though.

I'd continued training with Strong Style MMA, and their whole approach to training was different from what I was used to. I'd thought that was a good thing. I'd wanted to learn new approaches and new methods and to grow as a fighter. But as weigh-in approached that day, I came in heavy. I had to go through one of the toughest weight cuts I'd ever endured, even compared to my wrestling days, just to get myself down under the 135 limit in my weight class. And since weigh-in for that amateur event happened on the same day, I didn't have time to refuel after crashing all that weight. I didn't even have time to take an IV to rebuild the fluid in my veins. Which meant I walked into that arena feeling way less than my best, to put it mildly.

Plus, my Uncle Bob wasn't at the event. I had planned on having him there even though I hadn't been training with him in recent months. I wanted him to lead a prayer before the fight. I wanted him to give me some last-minute advice and a little pep talk like he always did. But he was sick and couldn't make the drive. So I went out there without my biggest supporter at my side, and without the completion of the full vision I'd had of Maddux by my side, either.

Thankfully, Brian Cadle made it. Zach was there too. He was pumped. He was up in the stands early, ready to watch me win.

Seeing those orange shirts, knowing just how many people in that crowd were on my side—that went pretty far toward taking the place of an IV and a good meal. I looked around as the announcer introduced me, and I took it all in.

My opponent, Jerrell Hodge, had just started fighting the year before, and he'd won all three of his early amateur fights heading into our matchup. But I'd won five straight fights heading into that match. I hadn't lost since my first fight against Nick Hyatt, outdoors in the rain. I had experience on my side. And even though I hadn't been back in the cage since before the night at Tammie's Tavern, I was still favored to win.

I tried to focus on all of that. I focused on seeing this fight as my very last amateur fight. I saw myself winning, making it to the UFC, and getting to the top there too. I had visions of becoming a UFC Champion, feeling Dana White strapping that belt around my waist, and hearing the voice of Bruce Buffer in my ears.

I'd spent the last few months fending off naysayers and doubters all around me, and sometimes within me. It wasn't easy to set those distractions aside, but I did my best as I stood in the octagon to dive into the wave of support I had for this fight.

Riding that wave in the first round was a breeze. I landed some good strikes and felt all kinds of confidence, but I was surprised Hodge was still standing when the horn blew. I didn't want this fight to go to the judges. I wanted to end it strong, but I never got the chance. I never saw my moment to go for the knockout.

Hodge came back hard in the second round, but I kept on striking the guy, and once again I could hardly believe it when he wasn't laid out on the floor by the end of that round.

I always try to stay levelheaded in the octagon. In between rounds, while I grab some water and get myself iced up, I replay everything in my mind and try to think what I can learn from whatever happened in the previous round. I listen to my coaches, try to absorb what they've seen from the outside, and concentrate on adjusting my strategy in order to get the best of my opponent. But on this night, with that huge crowd of orange-shirted supporters cheering me on, I'd had just about enough of this guy. I wanted to drop him.

I don't even remember what Brian Cadle told me as I sat there. All I thought about during the whole break was standing back up and knocking Hodge out. So when the break was up and the ref dropped his arm, I went for it—no hesitation. Within seconds he swung at me, and I dodged his fist with ease. I saw my moment. I was sure of it. So I stepped back in real quick, and just as I was about to drop the overhand right on him, *smack!*

The room went black.

I remember a few flashes after that. A medic kneeling over me. The muffled sound of the announcer's voice. The blur of orange shirts in the crowd. Staggering back to the locker room with my arm around Brian's shoulders, the faces of strangers all along the fence lit up in strobes of red and orange and blue from the arena lights. Some looked worried. Some laughed. Some cheered. Some booed.

I'd never been knocked out in a fight before, ever—not unless you count when Zach knocked me down the stairs in my grandparents' basement when I was six.

Hodge had thrown a lucky punch. I saw it on tape afterward, and that's all I can say. It happens. Anything can happen in the octagon, and it often does. When I came back ready to knock him out with my overhand right, he'd blindly thrown a right hook into the air that just happened to connect with my chin. That's the one spot on a fighter's body that can't be conditioned. It can't be strengthened. The chin is like an Achilles heel. Find it, and it's possible to cut even the strongest warrior to the ground.

I didn't fully come to until we were back in the locker room. That's when the loss set in. The embarrassment. The devastation.

This had happened in a stadium full of people. A stadium packed with people from my hometown who had come out and paid money to support Maddux Maple. I'd let them all down. I'd let Maddux and his family down. I'd let Zach down. I'd let my Uncle Bob down. I'd let Brian down. I'd let myself down.

I sat on the floor of that basement locker room and cried. It was crazy. I remember thinking how messed up it all seemed. "You start doing something nice, something good, and then this happens?" It felt like the whole world had collapsed on my shoulders. I couldn't breathe. I couldn't think straight.

"If I can't make it as a fighter, then what the *f-ck* do I do?" I cried. "This was all I ever wanted. This was all I ever wanted!"

"Dude, chill out!" Zach said. "This will all make sense in a couple of hours."

I didn't listen, though. I kept on crying. "F-ck," I yelled. "*F-ck!*"

"Enough!" Brian finally yelled back. Neither Zach or I had ever heard Brian Cadle raise his voice. "Enough of this crying, Cody. Get your ass up off the floor and act like a man. You cannot let one punch define you. This is not the end of the world."

His voice was like a slap in the face.

"You're in there fighting because you chose to fight, and there's a boy out there you are supposed to be a hero to, that kid whose name is on your shirt. He's out there fighting, and he has no choice," he said. "He loses his battle, and he gets back up and he fights again, because if he gets knocked down and he don't get up, he dies."

When Brian said that, I swear I saw Maddux's eyes. Those warrior eyes. It's like he was right there looking at me in that locker room.

"We are going to hold our heads up high," Brian said, "and we are going to walk upstairs—together—because we live to fight again."

Brian's words sobered me up. I stopped crying. I stood. I got dressed. Then the three of us walked upstairs together.

The next people I saw were Mic and Stephani. They were right there waiting with big smiles on their faces.

"I'm so sorry," I said.

"Don't be sorry!" Mic said. "That was a lucky punch. You were awesome."

"You were great," Steph added. "Maddux would be so proud. I wish he could've been here."

"Nah, I'm glad he wasn't. I let you down. I let everyone down. I'm sorry," I kept saying.

They both hugged me. It was almost as if they weren't disappointed in me at all. I didn't know how to react to that.

"I'm just glad you're up and walking," Steph said. "I was bawling so hard—"

"She was," Mic said.

"I was terrified that you'd really gotten hurt," she added. "I wanted to kill that guy!"

"Yeah, me too!" I said.

Suddenly we were all laughing about me being KO'd.

We were laughing about me losing the biggest fight I'd ever had.

Over the course of the next six months, the Maples became like a whole second family to me—a second support system.

I never expected that. When I started down this road with Maddux, I thought I was helping them, not the other way around.

I went back to Main Street Gym and started working out with Uncle Bob again, focusing on the fundamentals. He gave me some work laying concrete by day to make some money while I recovered.

I spent a lot of time alone, trying to get my head on straight and come to grips with that loss, but I found I was better off when I spent time visiting Maddux. He wasn't so shy around me the second or third time I stopped by. We smiled and laughed—a lot.

"What did it feel like to get knocked out?" he asked me one time.

"Not good," I answered.

"They said I got knocked out in the hospital," he said.

"No, no. That's anesthesia. That's a different kind of knocked out," I said. "I'm pretty sure the doctors didn't punch you in the face!"

We talked about Maddux's trips to the hospital and about how much he hated taking his pills every day. The doctors said he'd be on those pills for a couple more years. How could such a young kid fathom doing anything he hated for two more years?

Maddux also hated that he couldn't be in school and out running around with his friends. But he knew it was what he had to do in order to get better, so he just sucked it up and made the best of it.

As I spent time with Maddux, I got to know his sister, Makyah, a bit more too. She was a really sweet kid who'd been forced to take a backseat to her brother during his treatment, and I'm sure she wasn't too happy about that. But she seemed to be toughing it out just like Maddux.

I remember sitting on the Maples' sofa one day, watching Makyah and Maddux laughing and playing together. I thought, *Man, I hope when I have kids someday they turn out this cool.*

I wondered what life would have been like for Zach and me if we hadn't beaten the crap out of each other all the time. We have to play the cards we're dealt, you know? But hanging out with the Maples right there in my hometown made me realize how different life can be for different people, even when they're basically right next door. The little choices about how we live our lives, what we do, who we associate with, who we get into relationships with, how we treat those relationships—all of that little stuff adds up. Make a few of those choices differently, change a few little things, and life can be totally different from what you think it has to be.

Growing up in the 922 didn't have to be all about fighting. It could be all about love and support if that's what you wanted it to be.

You just had to make the right choices.

It didn't take long for me to know what choice I wanted to make. I wanted to keep fighting. Like Brian Cadle said, I wasn't going to let one punch define me. But I knew I needed to make some more changes if I was going to make it as a fighter.

For one, I was never going to let Uncle Bob slip out of the picture again. When it came to boxing, striking, learning to be the best fighter I could while standing on two feet, I knew for sure that there was no better teacher than him. Plus, love and support was the right choice.

But I also wanted to find a new gym. A few of the guys who came and went at Main Street Gym worked out at a gym in Pittsburgh, Pennsylvania, which was an hour-and-a-half drive in the opposite direction from where I'd been training at Strong Style in Cleveland. They raved about the place, and so I decided to check it out.

Fight Club Pittsburgh was a tough, brick-walled gym full of fighters with grit and determination. It was owned by a guy named Mick Morrow and his wife, Melissa, both really nice people who had big dreams. Mick was starting up his own MMA fighting organization called Pinnacle Fighting Championships, and he was looking for talented fighters to come get involved.

"If you wanna go pro, this would be the right place to do it," Mick told me when I first walked in. "I'm planning to launch in December. You could help us launch the whole organization. I'll get you on our first fight!"

I liked the sound of that. I liked the gym too. I liked it so much, I started to think that if I could somehow figure out how to pay for it, I might up and move over to Pittsburgh in order to train full time.

I was starting to chart a new path forward, a path that I might not have pursued if I hadn't lost that fight to Hodge.

Getting knocked out wasn't something devastating. It was a wake-up call. It gave me time off to reassess. And being around Maddux helped me to realize that.

Just because you're doing something good like I was doing for Maddux and his family, that doesn't mean you get a free pass to heaven or that everything will go your way. I had a lot to make up for before I'd get to where I wanted to be in life, let alone in the octagon.

This was only the beginning. And I was thankful to have a new starting point. I was thankful that God was allowing me to begin again with a whole new perspective on what I needed to do.

I reminded myself of what I'd told my mom: "Give me five years. Give me 'til I'm twenty-five." Five years is a long time. Five years was a quarter of my life at that point. This wasn't a sprint. It was a marathon. I'd stumbled out of the gate, and that was okay. It was better than okay. It was God reminding me to pace myself, to look at the long-term goal, to keep my head high and my thoughts focused. To stay on track.

I decided once and for all to ignore every voice that had tried to dissuade me from my goal—including my own. I decided there would be no backup plan, no second choice, no fallback position. No mining school. No more college applications.

I didn't know how I would find the money I needed to make training my full-time job, but I somehow knew I would. I trusted that God would have my back as long as I did right by Him. And doing right by Him also meant that I needed to stop selling drugs to make money. So I did.

I had the good fortune of my Uncle Bob's business, which provided work for me pretty much whenever I wanted it. But that was backbreaking work. It required long hours that took away from my ability to train. I was grateful God had provided it for me, but I also believed that He would find me some other work or a sponsorship or something that would allow me to focus on my fighting career.

I can't explain where I found that faith or why I found it over the course of those few months in the middle of 2012, but I'm sure it had something to do with the fact that I'd stuck by my promise to pray every day. The more I prayed, the more I felt like God wouldn't let me down, you know? And the more I felt like God wouldn't let me down, the more pumped up I seemed to get about chasing my dream.

I'm not sure that I'd ever felt so strong as I did when I looked in Maddux's eyes and told him we were in this fight together. And I knew the only plan I needed was the one I'd promised to Maddux. The two of us would soon walk out to the octagon together. I'd make it to the pros. I'd make it to the UFC. I'd be a champion one day. I'd achieve my dream, and so would he.

That was the pact. That was the promise. And I was sticking to it.

This wasn't about one fight. This wasn't even about me. Brian Cadle was right. This was about living versus dying—as much for Maddux as it was for me.

"Live to fight. Fight to live." That was my new motto.

Letting a dream die, letting it falter, letting it fade—that might be different from the death Maddux was faced with fighting, but it was still a type of dying.

I wasn't going to let that happen to me or to Maddux.

We were both going to make it.

Both of us.

Together.

FOURTEEN

IN MAY OF THAT YEAR, MADDUX RECEIVED A GIFT from the Make-a-Wish Foundation that allowed him and his whole family to take an all-expense-paid trip of a lifetime to Disney World. Steph shared the whole story for me after they got back.

On the first day in the park, Maddux stubbed his toe. He was just so excited and overwhelmed looking around at everything that he walked right into a metal pole. He cried a little bit, but it wasn't like he smashed it—at least, that's what his parents thought. He could wiggle his toes, and he got up after a minute and walked on it, so they didn't think about it the rest of the day.

Steph thought she noticed him limping a couple of times over the next few days and asked him if his foot was okay. Maddux said, "Yeah. I'm fine."

So they walked around Disney and Epcot that entire week, covering miles of pavement and standing in long lines, and it wasn't until they got all the way home that Maddux said, "I think I need to go to the doctor."

That was Sunday morning. They were in the middle of eating brunch together after arriving home late the night before.

"Why, honey?" Steph asked him, and he started crying.

"I can't take it anymore! My foot really hurts." He was bawling so hard that Steph decided to take him to the emergency room. The doctors took X-rays and informed her that Maddux had broken his foot in three spots.

"Of course I felt like a horrible mom," Steph told me. "His doctor was like,

'Well, when did it happen?' And he's like, 'Saturday.' And the doctor said, 'You mean yesterday?' And Maddux said, 'No, last Saturday.'"

"Oh no!" I said.

"Oh yeah!" Steph responded. "The doctor looked at me like he was getting ready to call Child Protective Services on me, right? I could tell he was thinking, *Oh, so you spent money at Disney and didn't want to come home early for the sake of your son.* But finally Maddux stepped up and told him, 'I didn't say anything. I didn't want to go home.' I was like, 'Thank you for saving me, son!'"

Maddux spent a lot of time in his wheelchair the rest of that summer, but when Dr. Hord said he was well enough to go to school, Maddux decided to go with crutches. He insisted on getting himself around without help. His bones were fragile because of the leukemia and treatment, and it hurt the poor kid to walk, especially now that he was a first grader in a bigger school with a lot more stairs.

Maddux didn't let that stop him or even slow him down. He just got up and kept going. He didn't complain about walking on broken bones, just like he didn't complain when he went into the hospital to have chemo dripped into a port in his chest. That kid fought matches that were bigger than mine every day.

"Live to fight. Fight to live." That's who Maddux was.

※

Carrying the power of everything I'd done—and everything Maddux had done—to get strong again both inside and out over the course of that summer of 2012, I stepped back into the octagon on September 15 to take my first-ever shot at an amateur title. This time I was scheduled to fight for the bantamweight belt at Caged Thunder 2 up in Akron.

After what I'd been through in the last fight, I knew I didn't want to endure another big weight cut the same day as my weigh-in. Doing that took too much out of me. So I decided to go in at a flat 145 pounds, a move that would bump me up to the next weight class, the featherweight class, on the amateur level. That meant I could potentially wind up fighting a guy a whole lot heavier than me, and that's exactly what happened. They matched me up against Clint Musselman, a five-foot-eight-inch, 155-pound brick house of a fighter with a 5–3 record.

That didn't scare me in the least.

Uncle Bob and Brian Cadle and I had set up a cage in an old horse barn that summer and held informal sparring matches with fighters from all over the region. My brother came back from the mine in West Virginia just to spar with me, and my longtime buddy A. J. came in to spar as well. It felt just like old times. By the end of that summer, I'd fought guys of every shape, size, and weight class and had held my own against them all.

Best of all, this time I would be walking into the cage with Uncle Bob at my side.

I was ready for Musselman. All I needed was one last endorsement.

A couple of days before the fight, I told Maddux face-to-face, "I'm fighting for you."

His immune system had recently taken another turn for the worse, and Mic and Steph wanted to play it safe. Maddux wasn't going to be able to walk me out to that fight, and we were both disappointed about that. But I wasn't going to let that get me down, and I wasn't going to let it get Maddux down, either.

"Don't worry," I told him. "I'm gonna win this fight, and I'm going pro, and you're gonna walk me out to my first pro fight in a few months, all right?"

That kid gave me a smile and a fist bump that packed all the power I would ever need.

On September 15, I walked into the cage and knocked Musselman out in the first round.

When the announcer handed me the microphone, I held up my shiny gold belt and told that crowd, "This belt is dedicated to Maddux Maple, a six-year-old kid, a friend of mine, who's fighting against leukemia. Maddux, this is for you!"

The crowd went nuts. Mic and Steph were in the crowd, but they hadn't sold T-shirts, and we hadn't made a big deal about inviting all sorts of people from Dennison and Uhrichsville to the fight this time. I think the Maples worried that all the orange-shirted attention had taken a little of my focus at the last fight.

I'd insisted that wasn't the case. I told them that Maddux was the very reason I was so focused now, that he'd given me the strength to get back up after that knockout. Still, they'd decided to keep this fight a little more low-key. So we were all surprised at how enthusiastic that crowd was when I said those words.

I think it really says something about the goodness in people's hearts that a fighter dedicating his win to a kid with cancer could instantly touch a whole arena full of people. I'd never been cheered so loudly for anything, and I don't think any of the other fighters that night drew that much applause, even the fighters in the main event. There was something magic about this connection. It instantly made sense to thousands of strangers in just a few words.

Of course, my first question to Mic and Steph after the fight was, "When can I give Maddux the belt?"

"What?" Steph asked.

"What do you mean?" Mic said.

"I mean this belt is his. I want him to have it. It's his," I said.

"No! That belt is yours. You won it. You deserve it," Mic said.

"No way," I said. "I couldn't have done this without Maddux. I want him to have it. It's already done."

I firmly believed that the belt belonged on his wall, in his house, to remind him of the many fights he'd won—and to let him know that I was fighting for him too.

Maddux was sick right then, so I had to wait. I kept texting Mic: "Is he feeling any better yet?" I was probably to the point of being obnoxious about it, but after a few days they finally said Maddux was feeling up to a visit, so I stopped by.

I handed him the belt. It wasn't layered in real gold or real jewels. It was just an amateur belt. But it looked just like those champion belts you see on TV. It was clearly impressive because Maddux's smile got so big at the sight of it, I thought he was gonna burst or something.

"It's yours, buddy. You won this. You deserve it. I told you, we're in this together," I said. "I'm going pro now just like I promised, and you're gonna walk me out to my first pro fight, okay?"

"Definitely," Maddux said.

Our local paper, the *Times–Reporter*, came and did a big story on the two of us, and that seemed to set the whole 922 into action. They ran a photo of me handing that amateur championship belt to Maddux, and suddenly people from all over came out of the woodwork to support him. The high school football team asked him to come lead the walkout onto the field at a big game. The wrestling team had him come out to be honored at a regional match. The basketball team honored him at one of their home games too.

The whole community seemed to want to get involved. It was amazing. If you'd asked them, I don't think anyone would have said, "We're looking to help a kid with his cancer fight." But once they knew about it, they stepped up. Mic and Steph were overwhelmed by the number of cards and letters they started receiving and the number of people who started coming up to them around town—at the Dairy Queen and the Dollar General and wherever, saying how sorry they were about Maddux's cancer and how much they were praying for him.

Things seemed to keep falling in place for me after that moment as well. After witnessing my knockout win, Mick Morrow, the owner of Fight Club Pittsburgh, made me an offer I couldn't refuse. He was an older guy who had done real well for himself. He had a nice house, and he offered me a room there—for free—if I'd come train at his gym. More than that, he offered me a job teaching little kids' boxing classes at his gym so I could make some money while I focused on training.

This was everything I'd prayed for in the aftermath of getting knocked out six months earlier. God had answered my prayers. And of course I said yes to Mick's offer.

Mick started going around telling everyone he met, "This kid's gonna be a world champion someday. Watch him! You'll see! World champion!" It felt great to find that kind of enthusiasm and support on top of all the support I already had back home.

Plus, I loved teaching all of those little kids. It was fun to get down on my knees and put the mitts on and teach them to strike. Kids love boxing, moving around, getting to do all the workouts, and it was a blast for me to realize just how much I'd learned and how much I had to share. It was so cool to be on the other side of those paddles, thinking about how much I'd loved learning to box way back when I was little like them.

Every chance I got, though, I made trips back home so I could pick up where I left off with Uncle Bob. His training was my secret weapon. So we worked on the Numbers with more intensity than ever.

And just about every time I got home, of course, I stopped in to see Maddux.

On days when he was feeling okay, I would take him out for a drive. I would bring him to our local Wendy's and buy whatever he wanted with the money from my new paychecks. It didn't cost very much, and it certainly wasn't fancy, but from his reaction you would've thought I'd taken him out to eat at a royal palace somewhere.

I was always on a strict diet, so I never ate fast food, but I loved sitting across from him in that booth and hearing all about what he was up to at school. It was hard sometimes, listening to him say things like, "Yeah, I just wish I could run around at recess." The thought of not being able to run around outside with my friends during those early school years was unimaginable to me. Recess and gym were the only things I'd really liked about school.

But every time we were together, I reminded him of our pact.

"It's like me training for a fight," I said. "I've got to be strict about my diet, and sometimes I don't get to see my friends and stuff. And sometimes it feels like it's taking forever before the fight comes. Like, I can't eat the Wendy's Baconator triple-cheeseburger and fries that I really want right now, you know?" And then I'd steal a French fry from him, and he'd say, "Hey!"

"This will all be over soon, and you'll wind up looking back and thinking how fast it all went—just like I will when I finally get back in the ring," I told him. "Besides, you're the toughest kid I know."

I told him that a lot, and it was the truth. I'd never met anyone tougher.

There were a few times when Maddux wasn't feeling well when I showed up, so I took his sister Makyah out to Wendy's instead. I just thought she deserved a little extra attention, given everything her brother was going through, and Mic and Stephani thought that was just the coolest thing ever.

"You know," Steph said to me one time when I dropped Makyah off after one of those Wendy's trips, "a few years ago, if you'd told me that my kids were going to look up to one of the Garbrandt kids, I would've thought, *Man, I must've done something really wrong as a parent!*"

I laughed. She did too.

"But you're all right, Cody," she said, and she gave me a great big hug. "You're something else."

FIFTEEN

I DON'T THINK IT WAS MORE THAN A WEEK LATER when I finally got to share the news that I'd been wanting to share with Maddux for so long: I was getting my first pro fight.

My goal was to fight guys who had way more experience than me. I knew a lot of other fighters who wanted to pad their records, but I was never about that. I didn't want to establish a 12–0 record fighting guys that were 12–50. My goal was to reach the UFC, to fight the best fighters in the world, and to beat them, so why not practice doing that right now? Why not challenge myself right away and level up? So I went and Google-searched whoever was making the most noise and was winning and who had a fan base behind them supporting them. That's who I went after.

I gathered Mic, Steph, Maddux, and Makyah in their living room one night and told them, "On December 29 I'm going pro. I'm fighting a guy named Chris Dunn. He's a huge favorite, with like six pro fights already behind him, and I know I'm gonna beat him."

"I know you're gonna beat him too!" Maddux said.

"And since you're doing better, Maddux, I already got permission, and you're gonna walk me down to the octagon!"

"Yes!" Maddux shot straight up out of his seat and jumped in the air.

"Easy!" Mic yelled.

"Don't break your foot again!" Steph shouted.

"This is so awesome!" he yelled, and he gave me a great big hug.

"Easy, easy," I said. "Listen to your parents. I don't want you breaking anything, either, all right?"

"I won't. I mean, I will. I'll listen. I won't break my foot," Maddux said.

We were both so pumped for that big day, we were sure there was nothing that could stop us.

But then came one of God's little reminders that this wasn't a sprint. Maddux got sick again. His parents thought it was the flu or something, but in early December Dr. Hord made the decision to readmit Maddux to Akron Children's Hospital. He was straight with Mic and Stephani. He feared not only that the cancer was back, but also that it might have spread.

It was time for Maddux to go back to battle.

I was in Pittsburgh, deep into the last weeks of prefight training camp, when I got a call from Mic. Maddux had gotten so weak the night before that his lungs had just about stopped working. "There was a big scene at the hospital while the doctors tried to revive him."

"Revive him?"

"Yeah," Mic said. "He . . . he nearly . . ."

I didn't know what to do. I could not understand how Maddux could possibly have been so sick that he nearly *died*. The last time I saw him, he was jumping off his couch!

"But he's okay," Mic added. "He pulled through. They're just going to run more tests, and we're just praying the cancer isn't back."

I fought back tears. I thought back to a year earlier, when I hadn't even met Maddux in person yet, when he was in the hospital and wasn't doing so well, and when I'd called and told Mic and Stephani that I would give all the proceeds from my next fight to them. I remembered how excited they'd been, and I thought about all of the local support that had come out for Maddux since September. And right there on the spot, I had an idea for something we might be able to do that would be even bigger.

Without even thinking about how I would pull it off, I said to Mic, "Look, I'm gonna set up an exhibition cage fight right there in the twin cities. Maybe we can do it at the gym at the high school. I'll fight, and I'll get some really great fighters to come out. We'll all donate our time, and we'll sell that place out. Every penny will go to Maddux and to cancer research, and we'll make Maddux the star, all right? We're gonna make sure Maddux gets all the care he needs. It'll be awesome. Tell him. Tell him for me."

"I'll tell him," Mic said.

"Tell him I'm gonna do that. And remind him that he needs to get better to walk me out to our fight at the end of this month too. I'm holding him to it."

He didn't answer right away. Then he said, "I gotta be honest, Cody. I doubt he'll be walking you out to that fight. I don't even know if he'll be out of the hospital by then."

I didn't know what to say to that. I felt so far away. "What can I do?" I asked. "What do you need?"

"Nothing. It's all right. I just wanted you to know. We'll get through this. Maddux is tough," he said.

"Toughest kid I know," I said.

I could hear in Mic's voice that this fight was wearing him down. A year and a half after all of it started, the emotional roller coaster was taking a toll.

I got off the phone, and I prayed for Maddux. I prayed for Steph and Mic and Makyah and the whole family. I know they were praying, too, maybe harder than they'd ever prayed in their lives.

I barely slept at all that night, and the next morning I woke up anxious. I needed to do something. I wanted to start making calls, but it was too early. I tried not to think about what was going on. Instead I thanked God for giving me the day ahead. I prayed for Maddux. Then I threw on some workout clothes and threw myself into my morning CrossFit routine.

As always, finding a way to focus on training set my mind at ease and made everything else disappear for a while. Then, when eight o'clock finally rolled around, I called my old high school. The secretary found an open weekend date on the gymnasium calendar. I spoke to my old assistant wrestling coach, Eric Seibert, who had become the athletic director at Claymont High, and we penciled in an exhibition fight for March 23, 2013. Then I talked to Brian Cadle and Uncle Bob, and we reached out to a fight promoter in Ohio named Dannon Svab. He started putting all the wheels in motion to bring in a cage and put a whole afternoon of exhibition fights together under the Explosive Fight Promotions banner—all for Maddux.

By the end of that single day, the whole thing was rolling forward.

That's when I finally got a call back from Mic.

When I saw his name pop up on my phone, I realized that my whole body was clenched up. My shoulders felt like they were up around my ears. I'd been tensed up like that all day. It felt like I'd been holding my breath for that entire time, and I was so scared about what I was about to hear that I almost let the phone go to voicemail before I finally picked up.

"Mic!" I said, trying to sound real positive. "How's he doing?"

"The test results came back," he said.

Mic's voice terrified me. My nerves were so amped up, it almost felt like I was getting choked out in a fight.

"And?" I said.

"And all of our prayers worked!" Mic said.

I exhaled and felt my shoulders drop, and the release of all of that tension I was carrying around made me feel dizzy.

Mic told me that Maddux's cancer screens were all negative. The cancer hadn't resurfaced after all. Maddux was just really sick with a bad virus. Because of his exhaustion and the overall weakness of his immune system, pneumonia had set in. But the good news was that his beat-up body was somehow finding the strength to fight it off. His oxygen levels were already rising. He was going to be okay.

Maddux got out of the hospital before my fight, but he just wasn't well enough to come to Pittsburgh and walk me out to the cage. So on December 29, nearly one whole year after I'd first sat down with Maddux face-to-face, I walked into the locker room at the Iceoplex, a multisports venue just outside of Pittsburgh, without Maddux by my side. I would be fighting as part of the Pittsburgh Challenge Series 1, put on by Mick Morrow's Pinnacle Fighting Championships. Mick was there. So were Uncle Bob, Brian Cadle, and some other members of the new team I'd started building in that city—but still no Maddux.

I hadn't gone home for Christmas or even for Thanksgiving that year because I was training for that fight. My family and friends had all bought tickets. Zach had driven in. They were all ready to watch me, and I'd worked harder than ever to make sure I was at my peak on that day. I had studied videos of Chris Dunn and prepared myself mentally for fighting him. I was ready.

Now the day was here. The energy of hundreds of MMA fans filing into the arena seemed to seep through the concrete walls. That normally would've been enough to get me psyched up, but I was finding it hard to focus, because once again things seemed to be going wrong.

We wound up switching around some of the matchups at the very last minute. Chris Dunn was no longer in the picture. There had been a few tense hours when I wasn't even sure if they were going to let me fight. Finally, the commission had allowed me to square up with a guy named Charles Kessinger, this crazy-looking dude with a Mohawk and tribal tattoos who only had two professional fights to his name.

So there we were, me and my team, minus Maddux, gathering in a circle in the locker room as I prepared to go fight a guy I'd just met. I had no idea what kind of a stance he used or what kind of a striker he was or what kind of a strategy I might want to use to take him down. I was basically going into my first professional fight totally blind.

Uncle Bob did his best to calm me down. He did that a lot before my fights. I'd get all fired up and anxious about something, and he'd talk me down and remind me it was just one fight. No matter what went wrong, he said, it wasn't the end of the world. Then we all held hands, and he led us in a prefight prayer.

This was becoming a ritual for us. It wasn't a prayer to win the fight or anything selfish like that. It was a prayer that God would keep me safe, keep all of us safe—including my opponent—and a prayer of thanks for the opportunity we had to go out there and face this challenge. Uncle Bob talked a little about Maddux—how thankful we were for his recent recovery and how much we wished he could've been there that night with us. But mostly he treated this moment like I was getting ready to go off to war, and this was a prayer for my protection and safe return.

The moment I started the walk down the hall toward the entry to the arena floor, I swear I could feel Maddux's hand in mine. He was supposed to be there, and I knew he *was* there with me in spirit. I couldn't let his absence cloud my focus.

A lot of my peers liked to play hip-hop for their walkout music. But this being my professional debut, I'd wanted to do something a little different. Something a little more memorable—a little more me. So I took it old school and went right back to the music of my high school wrestling days.

I figured there's nothing like a good drumbeat to get a crowd in sync. *Boom-boom, clap! Boom-boom, clap!* The opening beats of Queen's "We Will Rock You" blared through the stadium speakers, and I could hear the audience getting into it, stomping their feet and clapping to the music. It was just like I'd envisioned—minus Maddux, of course.

Before I knew it, the walk was over and I was in the octagon. I was face-to-face with Kessinger. The ref dropped his hand, and my first professional fight was under way.

Kessinger came out with this mess of a fighting style that quickly threw me off. In the first minute, he dropped me with an overhand right. He just caught me. Then he put me in a choke hold and almost choked me out. I could feel myself slipping. I nearly bit my tongue off just trying to breathe.

I fought my way out of his grip, but then my mouthpiece popped out. The ref stepped in and stopped the action. He gave me a second to put the mouthpiece back in, but I could feel my tongue swelling up and I was still trying to catch my breath and get my bearings when he started the fight again.

I realized I needed to get myself together, and quick. It was now or never. I had to give this everything I had, because this guy was out to kill me. In my mind this was suddenly a street fight outside Tammie's, and my opponent had a knife in his hand. "Live to fight. Fight to live." This was my life on the line.

The image of Maddux jumping off the couch popped into my mind. He was there with me. I could feel it. This was for *him*.

I started kicking Kessinger just to throw him off and see how he reacted— and he reacted exactly like I expected him to. I could see his next move coming. He did what I anticipated almost every time I hit him, and in that moment I knew I had him. So I hit him with a jab, a showstopper that was basically a setup to force him to come forward with his right hand, and that's when I hit him in the forehead with an all-out overhead right he never saw coming.

He staggered—and I winced. As soon as I hit him, I'd felt a pop in my hand.

The adrenaline was pumping so hard when he dropped that I ignored my pain and went after him anyway. I dropped down on top of him and started hammer-fisting him. I put my forearm to his throat and choked him, with one knee on his belly. Then it dawned on me, *Oh yeah, this is pro—I can elbow him!* So I hit him with three hard elbows to the face. He turned up, and I gave him two mean-ass hammer fists that bounced his head off the canvas.

He was out.

The ref jumped in and ended the fight. With less than a minute to go in the first round, I had won—a TKO in my pro debut.

I leapt up into the air and roared. I started bouncing around the octagon, raising my hands up, pumping the crowd up and feeding off of their energy.

The announcer called the fight and grabbed my wrist to raise my arm up in victory.

Then it hit me: *I'd won my first pro fight.* I'd taken the first big step toward making it to the UFC!

I looked out into the crowd and caught the smile on Zach's face. I saw my mom cheering. Brian came into the ring and lifted me off the canvas in a bear hug, and the look on Uncle Bob's face was pure pride. I don't think he would have looked more proud if he'd won that fight himself.

I didn't have a chance to tell the crowd that my victory that night was dedicated to Maddux Maple. But I knew that it was. Everyone around me knew that it was. And through the dozens of texts and pictures and phone calls my friends and family sent from the arena to Mic and Stephani in the aftermath of that fight, they were able to show Maddux that victory was his too.

The two of us were on our way.

SIXTEEN

AS I MADE MY WAY BACK TO THE LOCKER ROOM
after the Kessinger fight, I felt a throbbing behind the knuckles in my right hand. I grabbed it with my left hand just to see if I could feel what was wrong, and a sharp pain shot all the way up my arm.

By the time we got to the locker room, the pain was so bad I couldn't pull my glove off. I noticed some blood seeping out from underneath it. Uncle Bob cut the glove loose from the palm side, and when I turned my hand back over, we all saw it—a bone in the center of the top of my hand had broken right through my skin.

I'd hit Kessinger so hard, I broke my right hand.

Compound hand fractures are no joke. They don't fix easily. That break required surgery, and the surgeon had to put a metal plate in my hand just so it could heal. I wouldn't be able to fight again for months. And even if I made a full recovery, the doctor told me, there was a chance my hand would never be as strong as it once was. I would have to be "cautious," and cautious is the last thing any great fighter can be.

Any warrior knows that going into battle requires no fear—of death or anything else. Walking into the octagon with a fear that part of your body won't perform the way you need it to perform could mean a quick end to a career that had barely begun.

That doctor's words took the wind right out of me.

Just like that, all of the momentum I felt, the rush I felt, the excitement of knowing that I'd won my professional debut and was on my way to getting a shot at the UFC—all of that positive energy left my body. I felt like I'd taken a huge step backward. Not only would this mean I'd be months away from my next fight, it also opened the possibility that I might never be as good as I wanted to be. I knew that the mental fight it would take to get that "cautious" warning out of my head would be harder than the actual healing process my bones would have to go through.

I suddenly felt a huge void—the emptiness of doubt.

And what set in next? What filled up that void? What took the place of all of that momentum I'd gained?

Frustration.

Everyone around me was really worried. I could see it in their eyes. I could hear it in the way they spoke to me, trying to stay positive and not say anything negative around me. They all knew how hard I had worked, and they knew that I wanted to be better right now. And given my past history, they probably wondered if I was going to do something reckless.

But despite my frustration, I was starting to see things a little more clearly. I had learned a thing or two since my last injury. The knife fight at Tammie's had led me directly to Maddux. It had led me here, to winning my pro debut. I was hopeful that this was all part of God's plan and that maybe the downtime this injury demanded might lead me to someone or someplace else important too.

In the meantime, I had a great team around me. My pillars of strength.

Maddux reminded me that most of the time he'd spent in the hospital was kind of fun. "Just play games and stuff. Make the most of it!" he said.

Uncle Bob kept reminding me that "it's a marathon, not a sprint." He told me to keep praying and to keep my eyes on the bigger prize. And he did his best to convince me that God had told him I was going to heal just fine, so I shouldn't worry about a thing.

Mick Morrow and his wife were great too. They told me I could stay at their house for as long as I needed. And Mick never stopped telling me—and everyone else—that I was going to be a world champion. He said the broken hand was nothing, that I wouldn't even remember it in a few months. He personally trained me in the gym, working around my injury and advising me to take advantage of the downtime to work on weight training. Heavy lifting was his thing, so that's what I did. He encouraged me to keep teaching too. I did, and those kids brought a smile to my face every day.

There was this one little Russian kid who had more energy and strength as a fighter than even Zach and I did as six-year-olds. I loved training him. I could see the fire in him, the way he'd go at his opponents relentlessly until he won, and while he was standing there after class one day, I told his dad that he would be a great fighter someday.

"A great fighter whose first trainer was World Champion Cody Garbrandt!" the kid piped up.

It was nice to see that the kids believed Mick's constant chatter about me. I wasn't always sure I believed it, though. Even with my new perspective, frustration and I didn't go well together. No matter how many times I heard my brother or my mother or some local fan back in the 922 say, "Hey, you're gonna be fine. You're gonna get over this and come back," I would wake up in the morning, give my hand a little squeeze, feel the pain, and fill up with doubt.

I followed through on my promise, though, and set up that cage fight at the Claymont High School gymnasium as a benefit for Maddux. I couldn't fight in that exhibition myself, but we brought in a bunch of top-notch guys who could, and Dannon Svab put on a great event that March that got coverage in all the local media. Best of all, we did exactly what I'd said we would do. We sold every last ticket, raised a ton of money for Maddux and for cancer research, and had fun while we did it.

It was so great to see Maddux at that event, getting all sorts of attention. He was on different medications now, and his hair was starting to grow back. Seeing him on the road to recovery made me believe I was on that road too. I didn't understand why my body had failed me the way it had, but I hoped it was all part of something bigger. I also hoped that the doctors were wrong. I hoped that my hand would heal and be stronger than ever.

Having to pull back from a nonstop training schedule left me with too much time on my hands, though. And whenever I had too much time on my hands, it seemed like trouble had a way of finding me.

I started going back home most weekends. I'd stay with my mom and hang out with friends. I'd go see Maddux, take him out to lunch when he was able to leave the house, and it always felt good to see Mic and Stephani. I knew that whole family was rock-solid in their belief in me, and I loved our times together. But that still left a whole lot of hours in the day and even more free hours at night.

I wasn't looking for trouble, I swear. I just wanted to heal and get back on the path to chasing my dreams. But somehow, my going pro and winning my first pro fight caused certain people in the 922 to look at me a little differently. It's like they were jealous or something, like they had a chip on their shoulder and wanted to prove I wasn't all that—that I wasn't better than them just because I'd gone and accomplished something outside of our tiny little twin-city bubble.

I'd long since stopped hanging out at places like Tammie's Tavern. But even when I went up to classier places, fights seemed to come looking for me. One night my buddy A. J. and I went to a nice bar called Martini 97 in nearby Dover, Ohio. A big, obnoxious guy kept taunting us, and when his friends jumped up and that guy took a swing at me, I had no choice but to defend myself.

A. J. and I put that guy and his whole crew on the ground. I put one of the bar's bouncers on the ground, too, after he grabbed me from behind. As soon as I realized he worked for the club, I put my hands up and apologized. But they still kicked us out, of course.

The next day I got a Facebook message from a guy named Todd Meldrum. Turns out he was the owner of the bar. "I'm trying to have an upscale place," he wrote. "I can't have fights here. From what I saw it was clear to me that the other guy started it, but I just can't have it," he added.

I wrote back to him right away. "Todd," I wrote, "I apologize for the incident." I explained that I hadn't been looking for a fight, that I was trying to get my life right and that fighting in bars was the last thing I wanted to do.

Todd seemed real cool about it. He wrote back and thanked me for my reply. He said he appreciated that I was trying to make something of myself. He seemed real familiar with what life was like in the 922, and he admitted he had gone and watched a couple of my fights on YouTube. And then he said something totally unexpected: "If you need a sponsor or want to throw an event here at Martini 97, you just let me know."

It's like he saw right through the fight and actually saw who I was.

I went back to that bar the following week just to meet Todd Meldrum in person. We got to talking, and I told him some more of my story, and once again he said, "You let me know when your next fight's coming up, and I'll sponsor you. You put the name of the bar on your shirt or your shorts or something, and I'll make sure you have what you need. New gloves, travel money—you name it, and I'll see what I can do," he said. "Money's never really mattered to me. I just like to support people I believe in."

I was amazed. How could something so positive come out of me getting into a bar fight?

I had only one explanation. It was a God thing. Just as with everything else I'd been through, especially meeting Maddux, there was no question there was a higher power at work and I needed to pay attention.

God was reminding me that I had more important things to do than to get into fights with some idiot in my old hood. But God was also reminding me that He was there. That even if I happened to lose my way and mess up a little bit, He still had my back.

I went back to Pittsburgh and let my right hand heal, but no sooner did a doctor tell me that my hand was ready to fight again than I got blindsided by an injury that was far less visible. It was like every punch and kick to the head I'd ever taken in my life suddenly came back to haunt me. I kept getting dizzy. I got the spins. I wound up suffering from vertigo that would come and go out of nowhere. The doctor said it was likely caused by the repeated concussions I'd suffered in my life. I could only remember being treated for one or two concussions, but clearly I'd had more. With street fights, football, sparring matches, actual fights—you name it—my head had taken a beating through the years.

There were times that summer when I'd stand up from a chair, take a few steps, and completely lose my balance. I'd tip over to one side and fall down as if some giant had lifted up one side of the floor and knocked me over. I got the spins when I went to bed at night, too, and sometimes it came on so strong that it made me nauseous.

I went nights on end unable to sleep. I felt like I was stuck on the Tilt-a-Whirl at the county fairgrounds and somebody had forgotten to turn it off. The whole park emptied out and the lights went out. I was left there all night spinning and swirling and calling for help, with nobody there to hear me.

The doctors said all I could do was rest up and wait it out. It was almost laughable. There was no medicine I could take, no surgery that would fix it. I just needed to be patient. The doctors said I had to let my body rest and recover and simply hope that the vertigo would go away.

At that point patience and I had barely gotten acquainted, yet it appeared that God wanted us to become best friends.

The doctors forgot about one other thing I had to do in order to get better though. I had to pray. I knew that prayer had been working for me, and so I prayed. I prayed to God to let me live out my dream and fulfill the pact that I'd made with Maddux.

I had to make it to the UFC. I had to prove to Maddux that we could win.

Whenever I had good days, I made the most of them. I went back home and trained with Uncle Bob. I visited with Maddux and spent time with his family. I spent time at home, visiting my mom and taking my little sister out to the mall.

It seemed to take forever for me to feel a little better. Just like with my broken hand, I hoped my head was taking a little extra time to heal in order to make me that much stronger. I prayed that this injury and long recovery was somehow all part of the bigger picture, the marathon rather than the sprint, the big dream.

All of that positive thinking didn't eliminate my frustration, though. And the temptations still seemed to be everywhere. The devil was working 24-7. Always knocking. *Always* knocking.

So I turned back to watching movies full of inspirational messages in the hopes that they would give me strength to not answer those knocks. I watched *Vision Quest* again for the first time in years. I watched *Friday Night Lights*. And *Rudy*. And the Rocky movies.

I also went back to the visualization that had served me so well. I thought all the way back to the first UFC fight I ever saw on TV, and I pictured myself in the octagon, in Las Vegas, with Bruce Buffer calling out my name and Dana White wrapping the championship belt around my waist.

But in all that downtime, when I couldn't leave the house because the spins were so bad, the doubt and frustration kept coming back. It just kept coming back.

Why was this so hard? Why was every step forward met by a giant blockade? I wrestled harder with myself that year than I'd ever wrestled with any opponent. There were nights when I questioned what I was doing, whether I had what it took, whether anything I did would make a difference, whether I'd ever get well again or get to where I wanted to go.

It was Zach who said something that helped me finally hear and understand the answers to my own questions. We were talking late one night, and he said, "You know, your great fighters have always been people who really wanted peace in their life."

"What do you mean?" I said.

"Think about the books we read in school. Go all the way back to Achilles," Zach said. "Achilles was just on this journey to get back to his home. His shield depicted a peaceful time, like, a picture of peace. So this guy is fighting, but realistically—even Achilles, this unbeatable fighter—his whole goal in life was peace."

"Yeah, I guess that's true," I said.

"Nobody's goal in life is to just keep fighting. I mean, look at Mike Tyson or any other fighter who grew up in sh-tty circumstances. They weren't fighting just to fight. They grew up fighting because they had to fight, because that was the only thing they knew how to do well. But ultimately they fought because they wanted peace in their lives—a good wife, some money in the bank, a way to help their families, and such. And I don't think you're fighting just to keep fighting, are you? Sure, you do it because you want to get to the top and get your money. Who wouldn't? But I think it's more so you can get out and have a family and a better, more stable life, right? I mean, I know that about you."

There was something about that conversation that changed my whole point of view. In all of the visualization I'd done, I had never really thought beyond fighting. It was as if, because of my upbringing and my surroundings, fighting was all I ever knew. *But what's beyond that?* I started asking myself, *Why do I want to reach the top? Why do I want to be the world champion? Why am I willing to work so hard to rise up and conquer that goal?*

It truly was because I wanted to get beyond being a fighter.

Zach was right. What I wanted was peace. A good life. An awesome life. That's why I was fighting.

It wasn't any different than what Maddux wanted, I thought. He wasn't really old enough to know what he wanted to do in life or what his real talents were. But what do we all want as little kids? We want to grow up. We want to do something awesome, something we love. And we want to be happy. We don't grow up thinking, *Oh, I want to work in a dead-end job and just get by.* No, we dream about big things like being astronauts and mountain climbers and pilots and war heroes and billionaires and artists and ballerinas and world champions—all sorts of stuff that gets us fired up and excited. The fact that we start thinking about all of that stuff so young is part of God's plan, isn't it?

In addition to watching movies and visualizing my future during my downtime, I also read a lot. I picked up everything from the Bible to self-help and motivational books to *The Secret*. And I found that there were similar messages to be found in everything I read.

For instance, I'd been doing the whole visualization thing they talk about in *The Secret* since I was a little kid, long before I knew that book even existed. It's like we're born with these instincts to ask a higher power for what we want. "Ask and ye shall receive." We can see it and dream it and feel our desire for it before anyone has told us how to do that or why. It's just that so many of us get lost along the way.

I realized that summer that I'd neglected to pay attention to the bigger dream that was nestled down deep at the root of every dream I'd ever had. Getting to the top in the UFC wasn't my ultimate goal. It was just part of the epic journey

I needed to take in order to get to a place in my life where I had broken free of everything that was holding me down. It was my path to raising myself up, getting someplace new and peaceful and awesome. Something beyond anything my circumstances in life would suggest I was capable of achieving.

The more I let all of that sink in, the more I realized that I needed to make another change.

My workouts in Pittsburgh weren't specifically tailored to MMA. Mick Morrow wasn't an MMA trainer. He couldn't help me to conquer Muay Thai or jiu-jitsu or any of the martial arts that helped make the truly great UFC fighters stand out. He and his wife had given me so much, and I appreciated every bit of it, but the more downtime I had in all those months of injury and recovery, the more I realized that Pittsburgh wasn't where I wanted to be. My dream wasn't in Pittsburgh. In fact, there wasn't a gym or a team anywhere in my whole region that was dedicated to MMA with the sort of passion and drive that I wanted to be a part of. Even if there was, none of the teams in that region were my dream team.

I was done messing around.

My dream team was in Sacramento, California.

My dream team was Team Alpha Male, the team founded and led by my UFC idol, Urijah Faber—the featherweight/bantamweight pioneer and champion who had tweeted me back when I was just starting out and encouraged me to come out there when I was ready.

I'd also been in touch with Lance Palmer. Lance was a legendary Ohio wrestler who I'd actually wrestled with back in the day, and he'd gone on to actually join Team Alpha Male. The guy had encouraged me on more than one occasion to get my butt up to Sacramento and give it a shot.

So what in the heck was I still doing in Pittsburgh? Why was I still hanging out in the 922? Why had I not answered that calling? I'd worked hard not to let myself get sidetracked with fallback plans and distractions, and yet somehow I'd let myself get sidetracked all along.

Having that downtime for injuries allowed me to see with perfect clarity what I needed to do next. And as soon as my spins subsided and a doctor okayed me to go back into the octagon, I made a new pact with myself.

"No more BS," I said. "I'm going to Sacramento."

SEVENTEEN

IT WAS THE FIRST FRIDAY OF NOVEMBER 2013 when I walked into Ultimate Fitness in Sacramento, California, for the very first time.

To be honest, that gym wasn't very impressive to look at. It was stuck in a little strip-mall type of building with a small parking lot on I Street in this strange city I'd never visited before. Inside, there were blue mats wrapped all the way around the outside walls, with a little boxing ring in the middle and blue mats on the floor all around it. The place was nothing special.

I didn't care.

I'd seen some really nice gyms, and I'd worked out in a barn where I had to wear layers of clothing in the winter so I didn't freeze to death, so I knew that I could train in anything in between and be perfectly happy as long as I was working toward my dreams. And this was my dream. Ultimate Fitness was the home of Team Alpha Male, and that was the only thing that mattered to me.

Nearly eleven months had passed since my last fight. Because of the hand injury and the dizziness, I hadn't fought or practiced MMA in all that time. About the only thing I'd done regularly was lifting with Mick Morrow, who had accompanied me on this trip so he could "help me out." I'd never done any cardio with him, hadn't hit any pads, hadn't done anything except lift heavy weight for all that time. So I walked in there all bulked up, weighing in at about 165 pounds. That was thirty pounds over my usual fighting weight!

After buying my plane ticket to Sacramento, I'd barely had time to brush up on pads with Uncle Bob for one session—and that one session had wiped me out. "Man, I'm out of shape," I'd said, catching my breath.

"Yeah, ya think?" Bob had laughed at me just a little bit. "Don't worry. You'll snap back in no time. A week in that gym, and you'll feel like new."

By the time Mick and I made it from the airport to Ultimate Fitness, it was dinnertime, and only a handful of guys were working out in the place. But as soon as I walked through those doors, I knew. There was just something about the energy, the smell of the place, the vibe of the place.

This is it! I told myself.

This was exactly where I was supposed to be. I almost couldn't believe it. How did I get to be standing in the gym I'd been dreaming about for all those years—the home of the team I'd always wanted to be part of?

This was real. I was there. I could feel the adrenaline pumping through my veins.

"Can I help you?" one of the guys called over to me.

I put down my duffel bag. "Yeah. Cody Garbrandt. From Ohio. I was looking to do some training here, hoping to maybe join Team Alpha Male."

That probably sounded stupid. You didn't just show up and "join" Team Alpha Male. Urijah Faber screened guys all the time. He held open matches looking for great fighters all over the country. Fighters came from all over the world hoping to become a part of his team and got rejected left and right, and I was pretty sure this guy I was talking to didn't know me from Adam.

I didn't care. It was exciting just to be there. And in the back of my mind, all I could think about was that old tweet from Faber, telling me that he'd be waiting for me.

The guy who introduced himself was named Kenneth. He was a retired fighter who now taught a jiu-jitsu class and worked the front desk. He handed me a schedule. As I looked it over, I noticed that one of the guys on the mats was looking me up and down with a little bit of an attitude.

"Is Faber around?"

"Nah, dude," that other guy said. "I think he's out this whole next week. Isn't he?"

"I think so," Kenneth responded.

"Oh," I said. "Really?"

Mick raised his eyebrows as if to ask, *How could you not know this?!* To be honest, I hadn't even considered that Urijah might not be there, especially for a whole week. This was his gym. His team. I'd figured he'd be there unless there was a big fight going on, and there were no UFC fights that week as far as I knew.

It took me a second to recover from the blow of that news. I'd gone out there with such a big vision in my head, praying that Urijah would take one look at me in action in his gym and think I had some talent and ask me to join the team.

"Oh," I said. "Well . . . I'm here. And I'd love to get some training in. I was planning on paying for the week if I can. Anything going on tonight?"

"There's a community kickboxing class starting in a half hour," Kenneth told me. "You're welcome to join that."

"That's fine. Happy to get a workout in. I'll do that. But when's the next pro class?"

"Monday morning." He pointed to the schedule in my hand.

"All right," I said. "Sign me up!"

I dropped nearly four hundred dollars on the spot to pay for a week of training. I went through the kickboxing class just to stretch myself out a bit, then Mick and I checked into a cheap hotel and decided to make the most of the weekend. We got our bearings a little bit, driving around Sacramento with all its one-way streets. It seemed like kind of a confusing city at first, with all different types of neighborhoods. It seemed to change every few blocks, from downtown industrial to residential and back again.

Then the two of us looked at a map and decided to drive the hour and a half to San Francisco just to do some sightseeing. I'd never laid eyes on a landmark as big as the Golden Gate Bridge before, and with the trolley cars and everything, it felt like I'd walked straight into a movie scene.

I think Mick might have been annoyed with me for potentially wasting his time, though—on top of his already being a little bit annoyed that I wanted to seek out training at a gym that wasn't his own. He'd said that he understood, but I think he was afraid I was going to leave his organization entirely. I don't blame him. In the back of my mind, that's exactly what I was hoping would happen.

"Look," I said, "maybe Faber will show up, and you two can talk about putting something together. In the meantime, I'll see what this place is all about. I'll get to know some of the guys. I'll make inroads. And then we'll pick a date and fly back up here some other time. It'll all work out."

Monday morning came around, and I joined the pro workout schedule with Team Alpha Male. Those guys sized me up pretty hard, and I mixed it up with them for the next four days. I held my own too. Just as Uncle Bob had predicted, all it took was a few days back in the gym for me to start feeling like my old self again. In fact, I started to feel better than my old self. Those guys pushed me, and it felt good.

What I loved more than anything was that most of the guys in there were full-time fighters. They were dedicated to the sport. They lived and breathed it. Fighting was all they did. That full-time effort alone made them next-level fighters, and being in a room full of next-level fighters didn't intimidate me. It raised me up, made my blood run quicker. Even in the more casual workouts, it made me want to work harder.

I took every stretch a little deeper. I made every strike a little sharper. I focused in those practices the way I focused in a fight, with my life on the line. I felt totally energized and exhausted at the end of every session.

Mick and I were scheduled to fly back to Pittsburgh on Friday afternoon, so I decided to skip that last morning workout. If I went, we'd be cutting it close to reach the airport on time. Plus, I figured I'd be back soon, so what was the point? Mick agreed with me. He said it would be better to have extra time at the airport just in case.

But I woke up that Friday morning, gave my thanks to God like I always did, and immediately thought of Maddux. I thought about the way every day counted for him—how every day was a fight and every day was worth the fight. I reminded myself what a privilege it was to be in Sacramento working out with Team Alpha Male at Ultimate Fitness. It didn't matter that Urijah Faber wasn't around or that this hadn't turned out to be the big break I'd been looking for. What mattered was that I was there. I was in the game. I was pursuing my dream.

How many guys ever get the chance to do this? I asked myself. And I suddenly felt stupid for even thinking about skipping. Why would I skip the chance to train here for even ten more minutes?

So I got dressed and told Mick I'd changed my mind. "Come pick me up in a couple hours," I said.

"We'll be late getting to the airport!" he said. "What if there's traffic?"

"We'll make it. I gotta go. 'Bye!"

I ran to the gym, enjoying the warmth of the California sun on my face one last time before flying back to a Midwestern November. By the time I got on the mat to warm up, I was pumped, and just before we were about to start our session, I looked up and saw a blond-haired guy in a beanie come jogging through the front door. It was him. Urijah Faber was there after all.

All right, I thought. *This is cool.*

What was even cooler is that Faber wound up running the practice.

Suddenly everything felt like it was meant to be.

I'm not sure if Faber knew who I was or if something about my workout caught his attention. Maybe it was just because I was the new guy in the room. But after the regular workout was done, he put me through the gauntlet. I found myself in the center of the mat as one by one he called each of his toughest guys to take me on.

One came in striking. Another grappled me right away and tried to pin me in a wrestling hold. Another came at me with a spin kick. I deflected, counterstruck, and broke free of everything they threw at me.

No one said this was my trial. No one said this was my shot. But I knew it was. I knew that everything I'd ever dreamed of was suddenly on the line. I treated every one of those quick match-ups like they were a championship fight. I gave everything I had and left it all on the mat.

Next thing I knew, Faber put us all back in line, led us through a few warm-down exercises, and that was it.

"Good practice, men," he said.

As he started to walk off the mat, I went right up to him, reached out, and shook his hand. "What's up, man?" I said. "I'm Cody. Thanks for practice. It was good. Thanks for putting me with the tough dudes, pushing me."

"Yeah, right on, man!" he said. "So what do you wanna do?"

I was so excited that I just blurted out the truth: "I wanna fight in the UFC, and I wanna be UFC champion." Urijah didn't seem fazed by my brashness. I think he liked it. He stepped back and kinda looked me up and down. I was shirtless and sweaty, with more tattoos on display than any of the other fighters in that gym. And given how many pounds I'd packed on that year, I honestly couldn't tell if he liked what he saw or not.

"I'm just coming off a year layoff," I said. "I turned pro last year but broke my hand and had some health issues. I was one fight into my pro career and had to step back. But I'm ready now, and I'm here."

"Did you wrestle?" he asked me. I knew that Urijah had been an NCAA Division I wrestler himself, so the answer to that question was important to him.

"Yeah," I said. "I won the Ohio state championship as a freshman."

"No sh-t?" he said.

"I'm not sh-ttin' you. I gave it up after my sophomore year, though, to focus on boxing."

"Huh," Urijah said.

I noticed Mick come through the front door to pick me up, and once he saw who I was talking to he came right over.

"Cody's definitely ready to get training," he said. "I've got a fight lined up for him at the end of this month. It's his second pro fight."

"Then let's get him in here and get him started!" Urijah said.

"Coming out here's no problem," I said. "I've got to fly back home today to take care of some stuff, but I'm happy to—"

"Well, when can you get back out here?" Urijah said.

"Man, I'll be back here next week if you'll have me."

"Cool. Well, look, you've clearly got skills. And you won your first pro fight, right?"

"TKO in the first round."

"So here's the drill," Urijah said. "You keep at it. You go fight the toughest guys you can find, and you come train with us in between fights. We get you to 5–0 as a pro, and I'll get you to the UFC. I can make that happen."

"I can go 5–0, no doubt," I said.

"You know we work hard here," he said.

"I'm all about the hard work. Hard work is what I do."

"But we play hard too. Where are you staying?" he asked.

"Oh, just some hotel," I said.

"Well, when you come back I'll put you up with some of my guys. There's a new recruit I just brought on, and he throws good parties and stuff. We'll make sure you have a good time."

"We're trying to keep Cody away from the partying," Mick broke in. "We want to keep him clean."

"Look," Urijah said, "that's an important part of the recipe for us. Team Alpha Male is a lifestyle, you know? It's a whole thing. Some guys can't keep up. If he wants to make it in this sport and he can't handle the party environment, then he's not going to make it anyways."

Urijah then looked back at me and said, "If you get here and you f-ck it all up, then you're not meant to be in this."

"I get that," I said.

"Well, cool. Then I'll see you next week?"

"I'll be back next weekend, no doubt."

"Well, what about contracts?" Mick asked. "If you're serious and you can promise him five fights to the UFC—"

"I think we're good on a handshake," Urijah said. "You good?" he said, looking me straight in the eyes.

I looked right back at him and put my hand out. "I'm good," I said, and we shook hands on it.

"All right, man," he said. "See you next week."

Faber pulled his beanie on, popped in some earbuds, and went jogging back out the front door. I watched him go, and then it hit me.

My UFC idol had just asked me to join his team. He'd laid out a path for me to get to the UFC.

I was joining Team Alpha Male!

On the way to the airport, I texted everyone I knew to let them know what had happened. I typed like mad, thanking Bob and Brian and my mom and Zach and everyone else I could think of who had supported me so far. This was all because of them, and all because of God. I closed my eyes for a moment and privately thanked Him the most.

Mic was so excited to get my text that he FaceTimed back right away and put Maddux on the phone.

"Cody, you tell him what happened yourself," Mic said.

Maddux seemed excited to see me. "Hi!" he said. "Are you still in California?"

"Yup. I did it, man. I'm gonna train with Team Alpha Male!"

"No way!" Maddux looked at his dad, and looked back at me. And all of a sudden he looked real sad. "Does that mean you're moving to California?"

"Nah. Not yet anyway."

"Promise?" he said.

"Promise. I've gotta win five fights to get to the UFC. That's the plan. I'll keep fighting in Pittsburgh, and I'll come visit you. And you're gonna walk me out to my fights all through it."

"I hope," he said.

"None of that hope stuff. It's happening, just like this is happening. I told you I'd do this, and I did it, right?"

"Yeah."

"And you told me you would beat cancer, and you're doing it, right?"

"Yup!" he said.

Mic popped his head in front of the camera. "Congrats, man. This is so huge for you."

"Thank you. I'm just so pumped right now. Hey, we're almost to the airport, so I'd better go. Stay strong, Maddux," I said. "Strongest kid I know. I'll see you when I get back home, all right?"

I flew back to Sacramento the following Sunday, and it's hard to explain how unbelievably refreshing and right it felt to get up that Monday morning and head straight to Ultimate Fitness. It was like, *Wait a second. Oh my gosh, is this my* job? *Is this my only job this entire week—to come out here and train? That's all I gotta do? I love it!*

Back in Pittsburgh I'd been considered good. One of the top dogs at the gym. But here? I was green, and I was fine with that. I didn't walk in trying to prove that I was a great fighter. I wanted to learn from these guys—not just from Faber, but from all these guys. So I came in every day like an empty coffee cup, and I just started filling up with knowledge from everybody I could learn from.

I was there for a reason, and that reason was to become a better fighter, the best fighter I could be. So I engulfed myself in those practices. I watched what everyone else was doing in their workouts, especially the top guys, and I did what they did at the pace that they did it. I leveled up, and leveled up quick, from day one.

On day two I came in an hour before everyone else, took a steam, and did my own workout before anyone else even started. I was the last one to leave at the end of the day too.

Someone told me about a running track that wasn't too far from the gym, so on day three I got up and did a six o'clock track workout, then caught a steam and a solo workout at the gym before everyone else came for practice.

The thing is, I looked up to great fighters—not just in MMA, but in boxing too. I'd been raised by my uncle to admire the work and effort it takes to get to the top. And I'd read all about Mike Tyson, who used to get up at four in the morning. He knew his opponents might be getting up at five, but no one was getting up to work out at four, so he got up that extra hour early just to beat them.

I had a concrete goal now. If I was going to get to the top, I had to win my next four fights. No losses. That's what Faber had told me, and that's what I needed to do—period. So from the moment I got back to Sacramento, I kept thinking, *What can I do that the other guys aren't doing? What's going to put me ahead of them?* I just got it into my head that every day you're not doing something, your competition is getting better, which meant there were no more days off for me if I wanted to make it.

I had always fought my best when I went into that cage and treated it like a street fight, as if my opponent was trying to kill me. And now that I was here, now that I was rising, now that I was on my way to the UFC, I figured *everyone* would be out to kill me. Everyone would want to have what I have. Everyone would want to be better than me. Any opponent I faced might have the ability to kill my dream.

I couldn't let that happen.

Was it hard work to work that hard? No way, man. It was fun. Training with Faber and Team Alpha Male made me feel like a kid again. I woke up excited every morning. Every day felt like the first time I got on the wrestling mat at the Schottenstein Center. It felt like back when my mom would take Zach and me to a new wrestling club somewhere and we'd get to test ourselves against the best kids in the state. I got all of that excitement back—that love, that passion.

Urijah saw that in me too. He saw it and kept encouraging it. He kept telling me I had what it takes.

It was wild. My whole life, whenever a coach or a mentor told me something like that, I had listened. I'd believed it. And now Urijah Faber was telling me I had what it took. How could I *not* believe him?

As I got to know Sacramento a little better, I liked to drive around, and one day I happened to pass through the richest neighborhood in the city. The "Fab Forties" Section of East Sacramento looks like something you'd see in a movie, like the streets of Beverly Hills or something, all in a section of numbered cross streets between Fortieth and Fiftieth Streets. Mansion after mansion, lined up right next to each other. Every driveway crammed with high-end Mercedes and Teslas and Land Rovers. Every lawn perfect. Every tree beautiful.

I slowed down when I got into that neighborhood. I turned around. I decided to drive up and down each of those streets very slowly, just taking it all in and dreaming. I'm surprised somebody didn't call the cops, thinking I was casing the joint or something. But the only thing I was stealing was some inspiration.

It was all just fuel for some new visualization.

I was on a path. And that path wasn't about being rich—although, that would certainly be a nice side effect. I was envisioning what it would be like to get past fighting, to settle down and live the life of my dreams.

Those houses were all filled with families, and I wanted that for myself. I was sick of feeling lonely when I went home at night. I realized there was space in my life for a girlfriend. I wanted something more than those groupies and party girls I'd been seeing now and then. I wanted a partner, someone to be with. I was still really young, and I knew that, but I had dreams and visions of settling down. Finding a wife. Having that stability in my life. Why couldn't I have all that? I just needed to dream it, feel it, taste it, breathe it.

I started cutting through that neighborhood often, filling up on visions of what I wanted. I wanted to feel it, like I was already living it.

As for the partying that Urijah had talked about, all I'll say is that just as Team Alpha Male took things to the next level in the gym, they took things to the next level after hours too. These guys partied hard—and not just the guys, but the girls who hung around as well. I'd never seen so many beautiful women in one place, and they were interested—in Faber, in the team, in me. The temptation to do basically anything a man ever wanted in his wildest fantasies was suddenly right in front of my nose.

I'll admit here and now that I wasn't a saint. I embraced some parts of that Team Alpha Male lifestyle. But I kept myself in check, and I prayed every morning. There was no way I was going to let myself or Maddux down by screwing this up with drugs or alcohol or some drama with a girl. I had too much on the line.

The impressive thing to me was the discipline all of my teammates had when they partied. I don't care how much fun anyone had or how crazy things got, by seven the next morning every one of those guys was up, and by eight everyone was in that gym.

By the end of my first solo week in Sacramento, with only one week to go before my second-ever pro fight, I felt ready, truly ready, for the first time in my life. I thought I'd been ready for big fights before, but I hadn't known what ready was until I trained with Team Alpha Male.

Now that I was finally in the right place, surrounded by the right people, doing my best to live right and stay on the path while chasing my dream—in my dream gym, with my dream team backing me up—I felt there was nothing that could stop me.

On the Friday afternoon before I was set to fly back to Pittsburgh, after Faber had put me through some incredibly tough sparring matches and watched me come out on top in every one of them, I caught him looking at me through the black chain-link fence of the cage. He appeared to be shaking his head.

"What?" I said. "What did I do?"

"Cody," he said, breaking into a grin, "you're gonna be the biggest thing."

"Come on," I said. I didn't know how to react to that. It didn't seem possible that Faber could be saying something like that to me in real life. I tried to deflect it and change the subject. "Man, I don't want to leave. I've got so much to learn. I feel like I'm just gettin' started and I—"

"No," he said. "Forget about this fight. You're more than ready for this fight, and you know it. You're beyond ready. You've already won. I mean it, man, and I don't say this to just anyone. You are gonna be *big*."

EIGHTEEN

I FLEW BACK TO PITTSBURGH WITH LESS THAN A week to settle in and get myself acclimated both to the colder weather and to the logistics of working out at a gym that no longer felt like my home. Reality set in quick, and one thing was clear: I certainly wasn't big yet.

I was out of money, for one thing. The plane tickets, the gym membership, and trying to keep up with the Team Alpha Male crew had eaten up every free dollar I had, even after getting some additional help from Todd Meldrum. I *needed* to win this next fight—not just to continue my climb toward the UFC, but to make enough money to get my butt back to Sacramento.

As fight night approached, I also had to acclimate myself to the idea that Maddux wasn't going to be able to walk me out to this fight, either. Mic texted me that Thursday that Maddux was out of school and home sick again, and he was really upset about it.

I FaceTimed Maddux and I gave him a pep talk. "It's all right, man. We'll get 'em next time. Remember, this isn't a sprint; it's a marathon. So you just keep going. I'm gonna win this fight, and I'm gonna win the next one, and you're gonna feel better. I told you I've gotta make five in a row, right?"

"Yeah." Maddux looked kind of tired. I was worried about him. But I didn't want to let that show, so I stayed totally positive and focused on that call.

"Faber's gonna set us up at the UFC, just like I promised you. Me and you, Maddux. We're going all the way, kid. Me and you."

"Do you think I'll get to meet him?" Maddux asked.

"Meet who?"

"Urijah Faber."

I wasn't aware that Maddux really knew who Urijah Faber was. It was cool to me that he was starting to really follow MMA and get into the sport.

"Oh man—no doubt!" I said. "I told Urijah all about you, and he can't wait to meet you."

"Really?" And just like that, Maddux was beaming.

I *had* mentioned Maddux to Faber, and he'd thought it was cool that I was helping this family, and he really had said he wanted to meet Maddux. He'd asked about my family too. He was curious about my Uncle Bob and the whole Numbers thing. He'd wanted to know about my mom. He was way more down to earth than I'd ever expected.

"When the time is right, you'll meet all these guys. After all, you're gonna be walking me out to the UFC, Maddux. Don't forget that. You're as big a part of my team as anyone."

"Cool!" he said.

Seeing that kid go from tired to excited in a two-minute call made me surer than ever that I was ready to go in and win my second pro fight. There was just no way I was going to let Maddux down.

With the power of Maddux's inspiration and the backing of Urijah Faber's enthusiasm, I felt unstoppable. I walked into the Iceoplex on November 27 in the number-two fight of the night, going up against Shane Manley, a fighter who was two inches taller than me and quite a bit heavier. Uncle Bob was there to say a prayer and calm me down and give me a last-minute warm-up. "We Will Rock You" blasted during my walkout. I carried Maddux's fighting spirit into the ring with me—and I knocked Manley out with a whole minute left to go in the first round.

I called Faber as soon as I left the arena. "I won my fight—KO, first round," I told him.

"Right on!"

I told him I'd fly back in a week, and I would have flown back even sooner if I could, but I wanted to get my next fight lined up before I left town. I wanted to know that it was set in stone, so I'd be sure I could make enough money to fly back to Sacramento to continue training. I also had interest from a whole bunch of new sponsors who wanted to get their logos on my shorts, and I needed time to work with Mick and Uncle Bob to sort that all out.

I wanted to make my next fight as big as it could possibly be—to test myself and see if I was really ready for the big time. To me that meant taking on the best fighter in my region. And the best fighter in my weight class at that time was a guy named Dominic Mazzotta.

Mazzotta was a hometown Pittsburgh guy, and I'd been gunning for him for a while. At that point he was three fights into his pro career, and he was undefeated. I knew he had a huge following, and I wanted to capitalize on that, too, to increase my visibility in the sport. So I kept egging him on, calling him out on social media, until he basically had no choice but to face me.

We set the fight for March 15, 2014. "Mazzotta vs. Garbrandt" was billed as the headline fight of the night for an event called Gladiators of the Cage: The North Shore's Rise to Power 4. The showdown would take place at Stage AE, the twenty-four-hundred-seat American Eagle indoor concert venue in Pittsburgh's North Shore neighborhood—right smack dab in the center of Mazzotta's home turf.

I was psyched. This was gonna be one hell of a fight.

By the time I was able to get myself back out to Sacramento, I only had four weeks to prepare. That meant working twice as hard as ever before—and I loved every second of it.

I guess I've always been in love with the grind. My mom gets credit for instilling that in me back when me and Zach first started wrestling, but the injuries I had to overcome had given me a new appreciation for it. I'd gained the mentality of knowing that any day I trained could be my last. So I pushed myself and challenged myself that much harder, knowing that I could tear a knee or even break my neck at any point.

I met a kid at Ultimate Fitness who'd been fighting and landed on his neck wrong. He was paralyzed, but he still came to the gym. He'd been a star athlete and set to be a really good fighter until that freak accident happened. Stories like his always put things into perspective for me. Knowing that any day could be the last time I get to step on those mats made every day matter more.

I treated my time at Ultimate Fitness like a job. As fighters, we might not be clocking in every day and getting a paycheck every week. But if we *didn't* clock in and do the work every day, there was no way we'd ever get paid from our fights.

It drove me nuts to see guys who showed up late or skipped practice altogether. If they did that at any other job, they'd get fired. And I guess they did get fired in a way—eventually.

The way you get fired in this job is you get knocked out. You get in the octagon, and your lack of discipline causes you to lose fights, so you drop further and further down the card, and you barely get paid or don't get paid at all for the work you did. And eventually you have no choice but to quit.

I'd get worried about that sometimes. The money I made from those early pro fights ran out after a month in Sacramento. If it wasn't for Todd Meldrum and the support of a handful of other sponsors from back home—including my first-ever amateur sponsor, a guy named Jeff Brown of Brown's Heating and Cooling—I never could have kept training out there for my third fight. Their support is what covered my rent in "the block," a neighborhood full of properties where all of the Team Alpha Male fighters lived.

"Stop worrying about the money, man," Faber would say. "The money will come. Just focus on what you're doing."

Faber owned all the properties on the block, and in the coming months I'd find that if I had to be a little late with rent sometimes, he would let it slide like it was no big deal. He believed that I was going to be a champion fighter and that I'd be good for the money eventually.

The fact is, it's nearly impossible to make a living as a fighter unless you get to the top. A low-level pro fight might only make you a few thousand dollars. And if you only fight a couple, maybe three times a year, that pretty much leaves you *way* under the poverty line. So I knew I had to do the grind harder than everybody else if I wanted to ever get to the "after fighting" part of my dream.

I flew home from Sacramento a little early to get ready for the Mazzotta fight. I wanted to get in some old-school striking training with Uncle Bob before I went into that match. The two of us had a blast in the gym, just like it was old times. He was blown away by how much my fighting had improved since I'd gone up to Sacramento, and as we worked through the Numbers he seemed impressed by how much speed I'd developed since the last time we'd worked together.

"Sh-t, Cody," he said. "Mazzotta's not gonna know what hit him."

Another reason I came back early is that I wanted to spend some time with Maddux. Actual face-to-face time, not FaceTime.

Maddux was a little older now and his parents had gotten him a phone of his own. That's how we usually kept in touch. On top of FaceTiming now and then, he and I texted each other just about every day. It was usually just a "Hey, what's up? How's school?" and "How's training going?" kind of thing, or sometimes a "Miss you," "Can't wait to see you!" sort of check-in. And we used Snapchat a lot. I'd snap some pics and videos of me working out or hanging with Faber, and he'd snap me back shots of himself on crutches or in his wheelchair, out on the playground and hanging out with his friends. His health had improved dramatically since we turned the corner into 2014, and it was so good to see him making progress on a daily basis.

Mic and Steph both sent me notes during this time. "Are you sure he's not bugging you?" they asked. "Are you sure he's not sending you too many snaps? We don't want to mess up your training."

And I wrote back, "No way. I love it! Tell him to snap me more."

Seeing Maddux's snaps wasn't nearly as exciting as finally seeing Maddux in person, though. By the time I got back in town, he seemed like a brand-new kid to me. He had so much more energy. He was down to taking most of his pills once a week by then—every Tuesday night—and he always felt sick for a couple of days afterward. But he usually felt pretty normal by the weekend, and that kid hadn't felt "normal" for nearly half his life at that point. It was exciting for him just to discover what normal feels like.

The only thing that still bothered Maddux consistently was his legs and his feet. They were still really weak and sometimes painful, so he still spent quite a bit of time in a wheelchair. But overall, he was better than I'd ever seen him. And that meant he would finally be able to be with me on fight night.

"You ready for this?" I asked him a few nights before.

"I am so ready for this!" he said with a great big smile.

That night I gave him a bunch of brand-new gear to wear, including a new Garbrandt shirt with "Martini 97" emblazoned on the back alongside the "Madd About Maddux" slogan and the prominent "922." I gave him a set of Garbrandt sweatpants too.

"I can't wait. I can't wait!" he said.

Martini 97's logo wound up a little bit buried on my shorts that night, because so many other sponsors caught wind of my success and my move to Team Alpha Male and wanted to climb on board. Todd didn't mind one bit. He was just happy for my success and glad to know that I was pulling in some extra income. He let me know that he would be there in the audience that night, and I'm pretty sure that was the first time he'd meet my mom and Zach and a whole bunch of my other friends and family.

The energy from the twenty-four-hundred MMA fans filling every seat radiated through the walls as Mic wheeled Maddux into the locker room that night. Mazzotta and I basically split the arena with our fans. Together, we sold that place out, and all of his fans were on one side, and mine on the other, so it felt like a bigger version of an old-school street brawl.

I'd never seen Maddux so wide-eyed with excitement, and I think I was even more excited than him. We were doing this! After all the ups and downs, the injuries, the setbacks, Maddux's near-death experience in the hospital—all of it—my vision was finally coming together.

Uncle Bob taped my gloves and got me warmed up. Then we all circled up, Mic and Maddux included, and Bob led us in our prefight prayer.

At go time, Maddux stood up from his wheelchair. I saw him grab his right leg and rub it and lift it at the knee a little bit, like it was hurting him.

"He says he wants to walk," Mic said.

"It's okay, buddy," I said to him. "I'll push you down. We'll pop some wheelies on the way."

"Nah," Maddux said. "I'm good, I'm good. I've been waiting for this. I'm ready."

I certainly wasn't going to deny the kid what he wanted, and neither was Mic or anyone else.

As the big moment approached, I tried to stay focused on what an incredible moment this was. My third pro fight. Maddux's first walkout. One more step toward achieving the big visions and dreams I had in my head.

We stepped into the hallway, and I took Maddux's hand. I looked down at him, and I couldn't believe how focused he was. He was raring to go, like a pent-up lion ready to break from his cage, and he squeezed my hand hard when my music started playing.

Boom-boom, clap! Boom-boom, clap! I could hardly believe it, but that Mazzotta-loving hometown Pittsburgh crowd started stomping and clapping along. That old-school song was doing exactly what I wanted it to do, even though I was the underdog coming after the undefeated fighter on his own turf.

The thing I didn't realize about this particular fight was that nothing—not even a great song—was going to get that Pittsburgh hometown crowd in sync with me. There were a whole lot of Mazzotta fans in that audience who'd paid good money to watch him kick my ass. So when the announcer said my name and Maddux and I stepped into that arena, half of the people in the place stopped clapping—and started booing. They started shouting and flipping us off!

That pissed me off. Here I was with a little kid battling cancer, and this crowd was acting like a bunch of animals.

I was worried how Maddux might react to that. It was his first time at a fight, let alone walking into a stadium half full of angry people, and I didn't want him to be scared. But when I looked at him, he was staring straight ahead at that cage, burning a hole through all of that anger. He'd been gearing up for this walk for a long time, and apparently there was nothing that was going to steal his focus. I'm talking dead focus. Laser vision.

He looked so strong and proud that just looking at him got me more fired up than I already was. By the time we reached the cage, I was heated, man. There was no way that crowd was going to bring me down. I used their negative energy to give me more strength.

As the announcer listed off the names of the ref and the keeper of the bell and Uncle Bob gave me his final pep talk, I heard Maddux call out, "You got this, Cody!"

You got this, Cody. You got this.

When the announcer finally called out my name and said that I was fighting "for Team Alpha Male," the crowd booed even louder than they had during my walkout. So what did I do? I put my glove up to my ear, like I wanted to hear more. I *did* want to hear more! I started pacing back and forth, feeding off of that crowd, knowing I was more ready than I'd ever been for any fight.

Mazzotta stood way off in his corner when they announced him, and I stared him down, watching every twitch, every breath he took. I sized him up, and I saw him grin a little bit, like he thought this was gonna be an easy fight or something. Like having the hometown crowd on his side was all it was gonna take to take me down.

When the ref called us in for instructions, I pounced. I walked in fast and put my forehead right up on top of Mazzotta's face.

"Back up. Back up!" the ref said. I did, but I still stared that kid down, and he felt it. He kept looking down at the floor, not looking me in the eye. He suddenly seemed a little scared to me, and I was so positive that I was gonna win that fight that I decided I didn't want to do it quickly. I decided right then and there to hold a little something back for most of the first round. I wanted to test this guy, see what he had to offer and see if I could anticipate what he was gonna do. I wanted to test my reflexes under the pressure and the lights and the boos of the crowd every time I ducked a swing or threw a punch. So I would stretch this thing out, go the full five minutes, and find out how it felt to be in total control.

Mazzotta was a hell of a fighter—calm and cool and collected. I could see why he was undefeated so far as a pro. There was no question that he was one of the toughest fighters I'd faced in the octagon. But after sparring with Faber and his handpicked pro team on a daily basis, I almost felt like this match was proceeding in slow motion.

I threw more kicks than I usually would, knowing that Mazzotta was a jiu-jitsu-trained fighter. I wanted to come at him with some of his own stuff. But I was also watching the way he moved so I could anticipate where he was going. A twitch of a muscle in his shoulder showed when a punch was coming. A shift in his head signaled a kick. I could track his eyes and know where he was aiming. I had more techniques than ever, and they gave me the confidence that I could slip out of almost any hold he might try.

I slipped early on and fell back on the mat, and the crowd let out a whoop as if Mazzotta had been the cause of my fall. But I knew better. I popped right back up, and when we tangled up against the cage a few seconds later, I swept Mazzotta's leg out and took him down for real. I could have finished that fight right there, and I knew it, but I backed off.

I dialed it back a little too far then, and Mazzotta landed a couple of solid strikes to my face. But that only made me mad. Actually, I liked the way those punches felt. They let me know that I was stronger than ever. He nearly caught me with a knee to the face, though, and I realized I needed to stay focused.

One of us was bleeding by now. I wasn't sure which one, but the sight of blood on Mazzotta's shoulder fired me up. I saw the opportunity to take him down again, and I did, then hit him hard when he tried to get back up.

He switched to a lefty stance, and I wasn't even fazed by it. I kept kicking his shin again and again. I saw he wasn't looking for that, and I just kept taking advantage of the fact that he wasn't looking.

I guess he thought I was just playing with him or something, as if those little kicks were all I had, because in the last ten seconds of the round he opened himself up. He threw his hands back and started taunting me. I couldn't help but laugh. It was comical to me. I just backed up and looked him in the eye and swung my right hand around in a circle like I was Popeye getting ready to lay a big punch on Bluto or something. I threw a big kick that purposefully missed his head for a little dramatic effect before the horn blew.

When I went to sit down for the break, I looked at Maddux, and I swear the only sound I heard in that whole arena was the sound of his voice cheering, "Woooo, Cody! Yeah, yeah, yeah!" Then, slowly, the rest of the noise burst through. The boos seemed matched by applause now, and the music was pumping.

I caught a glimpse of the scantily clad girl holding up a card with the number 2 as she circled the cage, and I thought about the parties in Sacramento and the girls I'd met there. Any one of the girls I'd hung out with there was as pretty as that beautiful model. In fact, the whole Sacramento scene felt so much bigger than this moment. Even this fight now felt a little small to me.

In my mind, I was already fighting in the UFC. I felt like I was already back in Sacramento, partying with my teammates and celebrating my Team Alpha Male win.

I looked across the octagon at Mazzotta and stared him down.

"Hey!" Uncle Bob yelled, getting right in my face. I stared into his eyes, and he said, "Finish him."

I stood up and quickly ran through a mental slide show of everything Mazzotta had thrown at me in that opening round. I knew what I needed to do. I went straight in like I was gonna strike him, but instead I pulled back and waited for him to come to me. When Mazzotta threw a punch, I hit him with a combo. Then he tried to use my own tease on me, kicking my shin, and the moment he looked down to do it I hit him with an overhead right that he didn't see coming.

I noticed in that moment that whenever he tried for my leg, he moved his hands away from his face. I don't even think he was aware he was doing it. It was like a reflex or something. So I spun around, swiped at his leg, and waited again. *Wait for it . . . wait for it. . . .* And the moment he took another stab at my leg, I pounded him in the center of his face with a big right hook.

Boom! He went down like a tree in the forest, straight back onto the floor. I could not believe how hard he fell. I hesitated for a second because I hadn't expected him to go down that easy. I'd honestly surprised myself with my own strength. But then I quickly bent down and followed with two more strikes to his head as the ref jumped in and stopped the fight.

It was over. TKO—just thirty-two seconds into the second round.

That was my third pro fight. My third straight victory. The sweetest one yet because Maddux was finally there.

I ran to the cage and jumped on top of it, swinging one leg over and sitting on the top bar, roaring at the crowd, putting my gloves to my ears, feeding off of their screams and their boos, raising my hands up and egging that crowd on. Some sore loser on Mazzotta's side threw an empty beer can at me. I was about to get really angry again, but that's when I caught sight of Maddux and Mic grabbing hold of each other and jumping up and down, looking at me and hollering with pride. I knew I would never forget those smiles. I knew they'd stay with me for the rest of my life.

This was their victory as much as my own. And that victory was all the sweeter because it was shared.

NINETEEN

I'M NOT SURE WHY LIFE IS SUCH A ROLLER COASTER at times, but after hitting the high of that walkout and win, Maddux took quite a ride on the other side.

I can't even begin to explain how angry I got when he told me he was getting picked on at school.

"What? By who?" I said.

"It's just this bully," he told me. "He keeps punching me in my port."

"He what?"

"He keeps punching me in my port and stuff," Maddux said.

"The port in your chest? The one they use for chemo?"

"Yeah."

"Dude, excuse my language, but that's f-cked up! Did you hit him back?"

"No, I don't want to hit him. I just told him to stop. But he keeps doing it."

"Have you told your parents?"

"Yeah, I told them today. They said they're gonna talk to the school."

Mic and Stephani talked to the school, all right. Remember when Maddux got tutored by a guy who just happened to be the principal of the elementary school, Mr. Page? Well, he was still the principal. And that's who they talked to.

Mr. Page went to Maddux's teacher and confirmed that Maddux's story was true. Then he went right to that boy's parents and didn't give that bully a second chance. He booted him out of school that day. Expelled him. Gone. He made an example out of the kid and made it clear that no one—no one—had a right to mess with Maddux Maple.

That Mr. Page deserves a trophy or something.

I told Maddux I was proud of him for not hitting the kid back. He wasn't a fighter in that sense, and he didn't need to be. I respected the fact that he was a peaceful kid. He loved what I did and admired what I did, but he had no desire to get in the ring and follow in my footsteps. When I told him stories about the fights I used to get into with Zach and other kids from school, he was shocked. He didn't want any part of that. Hitting and kicking just wasn't his thing.

I guess it makes sense, since every day of his life was a fight just for life.

A worse call, though, came when I was in Sacramento training for my fourth pro fight. It was maybe a month after Maddux had walked me out for the first time when Mic called me out of the blue. I wouldn't normally pick up my phone at the gym. But it was the middle of the day, and when I saw his name on the caller ID, I just had a feeling something was up.

As soon as Mic said "hello" and asked how I was doing, I could tell something was seriously wrong. Mic's a real upbeat kind of guy, but his voice that day was all soft and hesitant. It didn't even sound like him.

"I'm fine," I said, "but what's up?"

"Maddux is refusing to take his medicine," he said.

"What do you mean?"

"He won't take it. He's telling us he wants to die. He's giving up. We don't know what to do."

"That's crazy. Why would he stop?"

"I don't know," Mic said. "He started complaining a little bit the last couple of Tuesdays. Then he puked up his pills last Tuesday and had to take them twice. And then last night he just plain refused. We tried again this morning, and he refused again. Even after we got him on the phone with the doc to explain how serious that is, he just won't do it. He started bawling, saying how sick they make him feel, saying he's sick of it. He's sick of being sick. He said he can't take it anymore," Mic told me. "I don't know, Cody. I think maybe those pills made him feel way worse than he let on."

"Yeah, I bet. That freaking kid is so damn tough."

"Look, I know this is a lot to ask. But we were thinking, I mean, if you'd be willing to do it, we were thinking maybe you could talk to him. Maybe he'd listen to you?"

"Oh man. I'm willing to try. Of course I'll try. Is he there right now?"

"No, he wound up going to school."

"All right. Well, how about if I FaceTime him tonight?"

"Perfect. That would be great. If anyone can convince him, it's you."

"I'll definitely try," I said.

"Thank you, Cody. We can't thank you enough."

As soon as I got off the phone, my heart started racing. I got real nervous trying to think what I could possibly say to change Maddux's mind. This was my buddy. My little brother. Why'd he have to be all tough like that, the way he'd been with his broken foot? Why would he do that to himself? Had he really said he'd rather die than take those pills? I didn't understand why he hadn't spoken up sooner if the side effects were that bad. Maybe the doctors could have changed the meds or something if they'd known.

I couldn't get the situation out of my head all day. I couldn't focus. I left the gym early for the first time since I'd started training at Ultimate Fitness.

I waited until dinnertime, and then I FaceTimed Maddux.

"Hey! What's up, buddy?" I said.

"Hey. Not much," he replied. He definitely didn't look too happy.

"So, your dad told me you refused to take your medicine."

"Yeah," he said.

"Well, how come?"

"It's bad," he said. "I don't want to get sick anymore. I don't want to take them, but Mom makes me. She makes me. I hate her! All she does is give me pills all the time, and she doesn't know. She doesn't know how bad it is!"

He started crying. He'd never cried in front of me before, and he'd certainly never said anything like claiming to hate his mom. I could tell by Mic's voice earlier that this was bad, but I'd had no idea just how bad it was.

"Whoa, buddy. You don't really hate your mom, do you?"

He got real quiet. The tears slowed down, and he let out a big sigh.

"No," he said.

"You know she's just trying to help you, right? Did you tell her how bad the medicine made you feel?"

"Yeah, I told her."

"Did you tell her before last night, I mean? Like, when did you tell her?"

"No. Just last night."

"And this medicine's made you feel sick for how long?"

"The whole time."

"The whole time. Maddux, isn't that like two years now or something?"

"Three," he said.

I couldn't believe it had been three years. I might've got stuck on just how fast time was flying if this call hadn't been about something far more important.

"Dude, you just sucked it up all that time and didn't tell them it was awful?"

"Yeah."

"You really are the strongest kid I know, man. But look, you've got to tell your mom and dad when things aren't right. Remember your broken foot?"

"Yeah."

"Yeah! If you'd told them how much it hurt, maybe they could have helped you somehow. Or I don't know. . . ."

I stopped, suddenly doubting myself. I didn't want to overstep. I had no idea if there were any other alternative treatments or any way to lessen the effects of those pills. I didn't want to put any wrong ideas in his head or make him feel worse than he already did. So I changed course.

"That medicine's really bad, huh?"

"Like, reeeeeealllly bad," Maddux said. "I just don't want to be sick anymore. I want to be normal."

"Normal?" I said. "You're way better than normal! You're a fighter, man!"

Maddux didn't say anything. He just seemed so down.

"Look, you've come this far, right? Your dad said you've only got seven months of treatment left. And I don't mean to be blunt, Maddux, but from what I understand, if you don't take those pills, you could die."

He looked down instead of looking at me through the phone. So I kept going. "If you die, who's going to walk me down to the cages? Like, we're making it to the UFC, buddy, just like I told you. Two fights left. And you're walking me down to both of 'em. You're my road dog. If you die, who's going to walk me down when we win the world title together?"

He looked up at me when I said those words.

"I tell you what, Maddux. Like, you make this promise to me that you will take your medicine. You won't complain. You'll just do it. A few months, buddy, and done. You do that, and I promise you that I'll make it to the UFC and I'll make sure that you're at every one of my fights. And more than that, I promise you that I'll win the world title, and you'll walk me down for that too."

Maddux let out a sigh and seemed to be thinking about it real hard.

"You really gonna win the title?"

"World Champion, baby—you know it! You make me this promise, and you're gonna walk me out for that title fight."

"Seriously?"

"Seriously. Think you can do it?"

Slowly, reluctantly, Maddux nodded his head.

"Let me hear you say it. You'll take your medicine, you'll finish your chemo, you'll beat cancer once and for all, and I'll win the championship for you. Say it."

"I'll take my medicine," he said.

"And . . ."

"I'll beat cancer," he said.

"Annnnd . . ."

"You'll win the world title for me."

"Deal?" I said.

"All right," he said. "Deal."

"That's my man," I said. "Now go tell your mom and dad about our deal, and take those pills. I'll be checking up on you."

"Okay," he said. "Hey, Cody?"

"Yeah."

"I can't wait to walk you down to your next fight."

"Me either, buddy. Me either."

∼∼∼

I checked in every week, and Mic and Stephani assured me that Maddux had continued to take his pills without complaint. They thanked me over and over again, and I just thanked God that my little pep talk had done some good.

A month later, I was back in Pittsburgh for another fight—this time for my first pro belt. Mick Morrow put me up against the local champ, a seasoned fighter named James Porter who came into that fight with a 7–2 record. What no one in Pittsburgh knew is that I went into that fight with an abrasion on my eye.

I'd taken a stray kick during practice. The Alpha Male team doctor had said he really didn't want me in the cage until it healed, but there was no way I was gonna cancel that fight.

First of all it was a big one for Mick. My fight was the main event that night, and I wasn't going to let him down, especially because if everything went well it was the last fight I'd be doing for Pinnacle Fighting Challenges. Second, I was on a roll. I was feeling great (other than the eye) and I was excited to have Maddux walk me out again. I didn't want to cancel on him most of all—especially after I'd just made that promise to him. I didn't want to delay our trip up the ladder to the UFC.

That fight was also a matter of dollars and cents to me. Once again, I was short on rent money and short on cash, and I wanted to get in the cage so I could get paid and get back to Sacramento right after it ended. I no longer wanted to be anywhere else. I didn't want to be in Pittsburgh, and I most definitely didn't want to risk drawing any trouble by staying put in the 922. I wanted to live full time in Sacramento, where nothing would take me away from my training.

With my eye injury, I knew I couldn't last in a long, drawn-out fight. I also knew I needed to protect that eye if I wanted it to heal in time for the next one. That meant I needed to finish the fight quickly, which is exactly what I did. I sized Porter up in the first minute or so, then went after him with everything I had. I TKO'd him at just over two minutes into the first round.

My pro record was now 4–0.

One more to go.

The night before I flew back to Sacramento, I gathered my family, Maddux's family, and my local fighting family for some celebratory Italian food at the Dennison Yard restaurant right by the old train station, in the shadow of all of those streetlights decorated with "Dreamsville, USA" banners. The meal was casual and fun, and it was so great to have all of those people in one place at the same time—especially outside of a loud arena. Here we could finally see each other and laugh with each other, and I could stand up and make a toast to them all.

"I just want to say thank you to everyone here tonight," I said. "I would 100 percent not be standing here today, one fight away from getting my shot at the UFC, without the support and love of each and every single one of you."

I looked over at my mom. She had tears in her eyes, and that messed me up. "Stop it, Mom. You're gonna make me cry in front of all these people," I said. "I'm supposed to be the tough fighter here!"

Everybody laughed, but then I looked over at Stephani, who will readily admit that she's a really emotional person—and she started crying at the sight of me almost crying. "Oh, come on, Steph!" I said with a laugh. "Man, look. I get it. This is emotional stuff. We've all been through a lot, and we've all come a long way. We're all on our own journeys. I don't think you all realize how important every single one of you have been to me—and to Maddux too."

"To Maddux!" Zach yelled, and everyone raised a glass.

"He's the man. My little fighter man. And he's gonna be finishing up his chemo and walking me out to fight number five in just a few months. But we're all in this together, so here's to all of you," I said.

We tipped our glasses back and had one of the greatest nights I can ever remember. All of these people were my family now.

All of them.

And I knew I was going to be missing them soon.

I'd given up my room at the Morrows' house in Pittsburgh. I'd packed up and sold off a bunch of the stuff I'd been keeping at my mom's house.

I was officially moving to California. No turning back. And I knew it was the right thing to do.

I wish I could say it was all easy from there. I wish I could say that everything just kept working out and there were no more bumps in the road. But life just isn't like that.

We weren't able to schedule another pro fight for me until October, almost five months away. That felt like a really long time to me, and I still had a problem with patience. The fight was set in Ohio, which I knew would be a good thing for me. Both Maddux and I had gotten quite a bit of local press attention, and that meant we could draw a big crowd. But the timing just felt wrong. I felt like I was going to lose all my momentum before it was time for the fight.

There were nights when my thoughts would sometimes fall back to the old negative and worried places I'd tried to leave behind. I'd try to get my mind off of things by texting friends and family back home.

Sometimes I'd send texts to Maddux, but then I'd remember the time difference and realize it was like two in the morning where he was. Other times I'd call Maddux's dad, Mic, in the middle of the night, just to get his advice or get stuff off my chest. He always picked up the phone for me. He was real patient like that. And then Maddux would wake up in the morning, see my overnight texts, and send me a note back that made me smile. I was just so thankful to have that supportive second family.

It didn't help that I was struggling with some physical issues. My eye was taking awhile to heal, and I suffered a couple of back injuries during training that really got me down. I was blessed to have a team doctor and physical therapist at my disposal, but I hated that my body wasn't performing the way I wanted it to.

It could have been that my nerves were getting to me too. I mean, more was riding on that particular fight than any fight I'd ever had.

Here I was with Urijah Faber telling me, repeatedly, "You're gonna be a champion. You're gonna be huge!" But what if I wasn't? What if I screwed up and lost? What if my back gave out and I couldn't fight? With anything less than a 5–0 record, would Urijah still be able to get me into the UFC?

I didn't want to ask him. I was afraid what his answer might be.

I can't explain it, but every single time I got down on myself like that and let my mind spin over and over this stuff, Maddux would send me a snap from school or a text that would make me laugh. It was crazy. It happened all the time.

Did this kid understand what he was doing for me? It meant everything—absolutely everything—to have him on my team and in my life.

I called up Mic one day and said, "Man, I'm just so thankful for your son. I don't know if he gets it, you know? But someday, when he's graduated from college or whatever, I'm gonna take the grown-up Maddux out for a beer and tell him how much he meant to me during this whole time period. 'Cause no joke, man, your kid saved my life. He saves my life all the time."

I know my mom echoed that same sentiment to Stephani. Once she was finally in that good marriage to her new husband, Mark—a marriage that seemed destined to be a lasting marriage—she had softened up a whole lot. She had always had my back in her own way, and I think she'd been the best mom she could be considering her circumstances. But she'd been kind of a fighter herself when I was younger, and now she seemed to be mellowing out a bit with age. She had definitely gotten a lot more open about her feelings and stuff.

Mom went to Stephani after that dinner at Dennison Yard and told her, "I just want you to know that your son and this friendship he has with Cody—this whole thing saved Cody's life. I mean it. He was just one bad decision after another. He was ready to throw it all away. And getting to know Maddux saved him."

Stephani relayed that message back to me, and I told her I couldn't argue. It was the absolute truth. I don't think she knew just how crazy my life was before I met her son. But then she tried to turn it all back on me, saying I had saved Maddux by giving him a whole new hope and inspiration and giving him someone to look up to and admire and feel loved by—not to mention convincing him to take his meds, which he had done consistently ever since we made our pact.

Honestly, I don't mean to get all mushy and everything, but we all went through a period there where we not only realized just how lucky we all were, but we were grateful for it—and we said so. We were also grateful for each other, and we let each other know that too.

That is a really good feeling, and it makes me wish that more people would open up and tell each other how they feel. All of our lives seemed better because of the way we opened up these relationships and got everyone talking about the blessings and the gifts we all shared just by knowing each other.

It's like we all leveled up in life, and not because I was winning fights. We leveled up in life because we learned to give thanks. My winning fights and the other good things that were happening felt more like a byproduct of the leveling up we'd done.

Anyway, because of all of that love and support, I got through the ups and downs of those months of waiting. I got through all of it. The constant reminders of what mattered most kept popping up, and the injuries got dealt with, and the challenges were overcome. I found it easier and easier to focus on the tasks at hand, which meant grinding like never before to get into shape for that next fight.

Ten weeks out, I entered into fight-camp mode. A lot of fighters think eight weeks is the right amount of time for camp—the period when you sink into training with 100-percent focus, doing everything you can to get your body in peak condition for the exact day of your big fight. But for me, putting in ten weeks has always felt right.

Even with my ongoing back pain, there were times when someone would literally have to kick me out of the gym during that camp because I just didn't want to leave. They needed to lock up for the night or let the cleaning crew in so they'd have time to get the place ready for the next morning, and I just didn't want to go!

The more I learned, the more I fell in love with the whole art form of MMA. And it really is an art. I faced new challenges in training every day, and it seemed like the sport evolved every six months. Someone would do something nobody had ever seen before in a match, and we'd all watch it and be like, "Whoa! What the hell was that?" Then we'd all try to replicate it and make it our own while coming up with our own techniques and our own moves too. There were always new ways of expressing yourself in the cage.

Some people think that our kind of fighting is barbaric, that the guys who fight MMA are savages, and maybe some are. But there's so much more to it for me. When I'm training, I feel so deeply integrated in body and soul. There are times when it feels like I'm hovering, almost watching myself in the cage, and I can paint my own pictures and create my own masterpieces with my movements. There are many variables that can throw that off, of course, but in so many ways, I can create my own destiny in the octagon.

That's what I was learning in those months of training. MMA was allowing me to write my own chapters and create the story of my life. And Urijah Faber's training was instrumental in helping me learn.

I never knew this before I spent time with him, but Faber had used visualization as a tool his whole life, much as I did. He tried to instill the power of visualization in everyone in the gym too. At the end of nearly every class he taught or practice he led, he would tell us, "All right. Visualize it. Visualize what you want. Throw your hands up in the air. You're the world champion! You did it. You guys did that! Put yourself there. Feel it. Dream it. See it. Taste it. Smell it. Touch it. You did it."

Like any good coach or trainer, of course, he would call out people who were dogging it or who didn't push the limits to get where they should be. But it was those positive messages at the end that really struck me. He would share quotes from some book he was reading, just to keep us inspired, and do the visualization thing all the time.

Not everyone listened. Not everyone paid attention. Some guys would just start taking their gloves off while he talked. But I couldn't get enough. And I knew I wasn't at that gym by accident.

Of all the guys I could have looked up to in the MMA world, how is it that I just happened to choose Urijah Faber, a surfer dude from California? It didn't even make sense. And yet look how that turned out for me. I wound up getting to work with someone who was a great fighter—and was smart and driven and inspirational and cared about life and family and teamwork and supporting people.

No one can tell me that happened by chance. Urijah's place in my life was as much a part of God's plan as everything else I'd been so "lucky" to encounter once I started to pay attention.

In fact, want to know what the Alpha Male team motto is?

"Think big, work hard, stay positive, and enjoy the journey."

I didn't know that motto before I came out to Sacramento, but I couldn't have found a team with a better motto for what I wanted out of life if I'd tried.

Of course I shared that motto with Maddux too. I told him I wanted nothing more for him than to get to live that motto for the rest of his big, long life.

TWENTY

ON AUGUST 25, 2014, SEVEN MONTHS AFTER I
FaceTimed Maddux and we made our final pact with each other, Maddux
FaceTimed me with some big news.

"Guess what?" he said.

"What?" I said. "What's up, man? You look excited."

"I took my final dose of chemo today."

"No way! Really? So you're done? It's all over?"

"Yup. No more pills."

"Dude! That is so awesome!"

"I'm in remission for real."

"Like no more cancer? You kicked its ass?"

"Yup!" he said. "My tests came back clear. Again."

"Maddux! That is awesome!" I said.

"And guess what else?" Maddux said.

"What?" I asked him.

"That means it's your turn," he said. "I held up my end of the bargain, so
now it's *your* turn."

It was unbelievable. The kid had *won*. He'd done it. He'd reached his goal.

"I wish I was there to celebrate with you," I said.

"Me too. But you need to keep training. You're going to the UFC. I'm
gonna walk you down to the title fight, remember?"

"Yeah," I said. "I remember. And you know what? Just because you said that, I'm gonna go back to the gym right now. You've inspired me. I'm so proud of you, Maddux. I love you, kid."

"Love you, too, Cody. Go win!"

I went back to the gym that night and pushed myself harder than I had in weeks.

Maddux had won his championship right there. He'd technically been in remission for a while, but finishing the ongoing chemo treatments had been the key to kicking leukemia's ass. And now he was through with the chemo.

He'd still have to go in for checkups every six weeks or so for a while. And he wouldn't officially be considered "cancer free" until his tests came back clear for five straight years. That's a long time, especially in the life of a kid. He would be in middle school by the time he got to celebrate that milestone. But we didn't need to worry about that right now. Right now was a time to rejoice.

When I woke up the next morning, I had tears in my eyes. Maddux had done it. He really had. I thanked God for bringing us both this far.

I got out of bed feeling sick and tired of dealing with my back pain and the way it affected my focus. So, feeling newly inspired by Maddux's big news, I started looking for alternative treatments that would help me heal. I swear that just the act of getting off my butt and trying to find a solution to the problems I was having made me feel better. I'd been stuck sitting around in my own self-pity instead of chasing the dream. Now it was chase time.

I doubled down on my prayers too. I spent extra time every morning asking God to take care of everyone in my life and to bring me the peace I was searching for. I hadn't been going to church very much, but I snuck off on a few Sunday mornings and filled up my cup with the Word of God. Just as when I was younger, I came out of there feeling like the preacher was talking directly to me—like whatever sermon he picked that day was preached for my benefit. I listened, and I learned, just like I did in the gym. And that centered me.

But the thing that centered me most of all was Maddux. I didn't call him every day. I'd sometimes go a few days without much more than a quick text or snap, because I was so focused on training. But he was with me through the whole thing. He was my motivation, my reason not to give up, because this little kid had never given up. Never, even when he'd wanted to. I had motivated him that one time, and he motivated me back a thousand times more without even knowing it.

When my body was sore, I pushed on—because Maddux would've pushed on.

When I started to moan and complain about something, I shut up—because Maddux would've shut up and kept it to himself.

When I woke up feeling like maybe I didn't want to go to the gym in the morning, I went—because Maddux would've gotten up and kept fighting for his life.

This was *my* life. My dream life. And it was worth fighting for.

If Maddux got up and decided he didn't want to take his medicine, then he would die. If I got up and didn't take my medicine—if I didn't do the hard things, the uneasy things, the uncomfortable things, the necessary things—I would die too. It didn't matter if it made me sick. It didn't matter if it made me tired. If I wanted to reach the goal, if I wanted to live up to my side of our pact, then I had to pay the price and do it.

The everyday reminder of Maddux's battle is what pushed me forward.

After that awesome call from Maddux, I drilled down hard. I spent extra time with the Alpha Male nutritionist and followed the strictest diet I'd ever followed. I spent more hours at the gym than anyone else, period. I would get up early, like I did in my first solo week, then hit the track, catch a steam, and work out alone before anyone else came into the gym. I loved the routine of it all. My own schedule. My own routine that worked for me, uninterrupted by other demands.

As for my back problems, I found this place on the other side of town that had a float tank. I could submerge myself in saltwater in a sealed chamber and let every muscle in my body completely relax while I let my mind wander in some sort of meditative state. That, combined with some therapy in a hyperbaric chamber, almost magically made my back pain disappear.

The therapy was expensive—really expensive. But Todd Meldrum and his brother chipped in to pay for that too. Todd wanted to see me succeed, and when I told him I thought it would help, he ponied up.

As the time for my fight drew closer, we flew Uncle Bob up to Sacramento so we could integrate him into my team and work on my striking the way I wanted and needed to work on it. So now I had family there, too, acting as part of my team and part of Team Alpha Male.

I was flat broke in those days. I had nothing. But I had everything I ever wanted or needed.

God provides. He proved that to me in those days. When you're on the right path, when you honor Him, He provides.

In October I flew back to Canton, Ohio, for the first fight I'd had in my home state since I was an amateur—and the last fight I needed to win on my road to the UFC.

Fight number five. The last one.

I was up against a scary looking dude named Charles "Trinity" Stanford, who came into that fight with a 5–2 record. Four of his wins were by KO, one by submission—four out of five in round one. Of the two guys he'd lost to, one was one of the best fighters in the state, and the other was a UFC veteran.

Stanford was good, in other words. He was hungry. And he wanted to take me *down*.

But I was ready. I had put everything and everyone in place. My whole team was there. When we circled up and said our prayer in the locker room, we pretty much filled the entire room.

Ohio wrestling legend Lance Palmer, my old buddy, was there backing me up and acting as a part of my team now. It blew me away that he wanted to come aboard and share his knowledge with me.

Faber even flew down for this one. He believed in me and wanted to be there not only as a coach, but to witness my big moment. "You're gonna be so big!" he reminded me again, and I let it sink in. I was finally able to introduce Faber to Maddux and his family too. Just as I expected, he spent a ton of time talking with them and getting to know them—and vice versa.

The arena was only a twenty-five-minute drive from my hometown, so my hometown crowd came out strong. They booed Stanford when he walked out, but not because they didn't like the guy. He was one of the best fighters around and had a huge following. That crowd booed because they were all rooting for *me*. It was the polar opposite of what I'd walked into for the Mazzotta fight. I felt like my whole state was behind me now, and I knew that Maddux had as much to do with my surge in popularity as pretty much anything I'd accomplished so far in the cage.

I worried a little bit that Stanford might feed off of that booing and negative energy, the way I'd fed off of that energy in the Mazzotta fight. But Uncle Bob talked me down, like he always did. He brought me back to focus on what I knew—that there was only one person who could lose that fight, and that person was me. I would be fighting against me in that cage as much as I was fighting against anyone else. "And you got this," he said. "You know you got this. You're in better shape than you've ever been in your life."

I nodded. Uncle Bob was right.

"Maddux," I said. "Which hand do you want me to knock Stanford out with?"

Maddux thought about it really hard and then said, "Your left. I think it should be your left this time."

Everyone laughed, and I patted him on the head. "Left it is. You got it, kid."

When the music started and the announcer said my name, I was raring to go. It seemed like the spectacle and the show got bigger with every fight. The walkouts were specifically designed with cameras and TV in mind, and for this one, Mic and Maddux were placed with the rest of my team wearing brand-new "Cody 'No Love' Garbrandt" T-shirts behind a big banner with my name on it.

I got out front and nearly sprinted down to the octagon through the roar of that awesome crowd as a cameraman ran backward in front of me. It was wild. I wished I could have held Maddux's hand for that, but he was fine with the whole thing. He was so easygoing. He was just excited to get out there and be in the thick of the action, inches from the ring, as I prepared for the most important fight of my career so far.

As my shirt came off and I stood by the cage, taking those final moments to let it all sink in, I hugged and chest-bumped every member of that team—hugging Mic and then Maddux at the very end. I made sure Maddux was the very last person I hugged before I turned myself over to the officials so they could do their final checks: looking at my mouth guard and patting me down, greasing my face, checking my gloves and my fingernails before sending me into the cage.

While the checks were going on, I kept pacing back and forth—moving fast, staring Stanford down. I was ready for this. So ready for this.

We both weighed in at 136. We had the same reach. This was maybe the most even match I'd ever had, and this guy looked tough. It was time to test the waters.

When the ref dropped his hand, Stanford and I moved right in to each other, but neither one of us made a first move. I threw a little side kick and watched where he went. I landed a light inside kick to his front leg and noticed how he reacted. I sized him up with a harder outside leg kick and it knocked him off-balance, and that was pretty much all I needed to see. He tried to strike my head with a right hand punch, and I hit him with a body shot underneath. I could tell I'd hurt him. I felt him pull back, and I went all in. Right, left, right.

He came at me with a big right hook, but I ducked under it and backed him up against the cage. Then I picked him up and slammed him to the floor. I nearly had him pinned, but he kicked off of the cage. This guy was strong. He almost flipped me over, but I hung on and managed to stay on top. I pinned him again, but I didn't want to let him catch his breath, so I let up, and he jumped to his feet. But I still had my arms around his neck, and before he could break from me I kneed him to the face.

He staggered, and I hit him with a couple of body shots again. He staggered back some more, and I went for a full-on Urijah Faber–style jumping double knee, right up in the air. This was fun! My knees didn't connect, but I still knew I had him. He was hurt.

I backed up and let him come at me. He threw a left and a right and missed. I deflected a kick, then got my arms around his head again and kneed him in the face—twice. I didn't go too hard on him, but when he threw another punch it left him open, so I nailed him with a right and nearly knocked him out.

The crowd went nuts. Stanford covered his head while I pounded and pounded, looking to finish. I hit him with a head kick, but his hands were still protecting him. So I looked for an opening and found it.

This was it.

Maddux had picked my left hand for the knockout, and it was time to let it fly. I slammed Stanford with a huge body shot to the ribs, and he went down.

The ref called the fight. I was now 5–0 in my pro career, all by knockout, all in two rounds or less.

I raised my arms. I jumped up on top of the cage to celebrate with that crowd. I roared, and they roared right back. Then the whole crowd started chanting, "9-2-2 . . . 9-2-2 . . . 9-2-2. . . ."

The 922 stigma had suddenly switched into a prideworthy chant, and all because of me. All because of us!

As the ref called me to the center and the announcer stepped in to officially call my win, I noticed Stanford was still on the ground. He'd pulled himself up, but he was sitting with his back up against the cage.

I went over and touched gloves with him. "Good fight, man. Good fight."

He nodded, but he looked real down. I could only imagine how I would've felt if I was in his spot. It had to hurt—and I'm not talking about the pain in his ribs. I honestly felt real bad for the guy.

Then I looked out and saw Maddux, beaming, and I smiled. This wasn't a time for sadness. This was our moment.

I touched my right glove to my heart and pounded my chest, then pointed to him. "That was for you," I mouthed. Maddux nodded back with a huge smile on his face and a big thumbs-up.

One minute and thirty-seven seconds. That's all it took to end it. That was all the time it took to put everything I'd learned in the last five months of training—and the entirety of my life so far—to work to get the job done.

When the announcer gave me an opportunity to speak, I once again gave thanks where thanks was due. "First of all I want to thank the Lord for everything, for keeping me strong through the camps and just in life in general," I said. I thanked my sponsors. I thanked Urijah. I thanked my Uncle Bob. Instead of thanking Todd Meldrum by name, I said to the crowd and the TV cameras, "You guys want to come out and party? Martini 97 in Dover, Ohio. We'll be there."

As my whole team came into the cage for a group photo, I fist-bumped Maddux, knowing that I'd left that crowd with some words that would resonate all the way up to the top of the UFC: "I'm on my way," I'd said into the microphone that night. "This is what I want to do, and no man can take my dreams from me."

TWENTY-ONE

I HAD ACCOMPLISHED EXACTLY WHAT URIJAH
Faber told me to accomplish on the first day I shook his hand: a 5–0 record
against serious fighters. I'd fulfilled my end of that pact, and now it was
his turn.

Not even a month later, he came through.

On a whim I flew down to Austin, Texas, to support my teammate Joseph
Benevidez at a UFC fight. While we were there, we just happened to run
into UFC matchmaker Sean Shelby, who was trying to put some final bouts
together for UFC 182. The event was scheduled for January 3 in Las Vegas,
just over a month away, and thanks to my 5–0 record, Sean thought I might
make a good match for a more seasoned fighter named Marcus Brimage.
Brimage had twelve pro fights under his belt, the last five of which were UFC
fights. His record was mixed, but Sean thought that putting him up against a
newcomer with a perfect record would make for some good drama.

"You want to take it?" he asked.

"Yeah!" I told him. "Let's go. I'm ready."

"We'll have to wait to hear back from the other camp, to see if they accept
it," he said, "so don't get too excited quite yet."

It was too late. I called my mom about ten seconds later and said, "I know
money's gonna be tight because it's Christmas and everything, but you'd better set some money aside, 'cause you're gonna need to buy tickets to come see
me fight in Vegas!"

I was pumped. I was ready. I hadn't suffered any injuries at all in the Stanford fight, so I knew I could be ready in four weeks. No doubt.

Urijah followed up with Sean for me to make sure it came together, and within a week they confirmed the fight. Brimage had said yes. They'd put me on the bill for my first UFC event. I was going to Vegas, baby!

All of a sudden we were busy talking about the logistics and what it would take to get the team out there. And in the middle of one of the planning sessions, Urijah mentioned that my entourage would be limited for the walkout. I wouldn't be able to walk with anyone except my coaches, he said.

"No family?" I asked.

"Uncle Bob can come 'cause he's part of the team."

"But what about Maddux?"

Urijah looked pained to tell me news he knew I didn't want to hear. "Dude," he said, "there's just no way."

Not only was Maddux a kid, but I was a newcomer to UFC. I had to play it cool, keep my asks to a minimum, and just be a team player so I didn't come across like a pain in the ass. I would be way down the card that night. I didn't have a huge fan base. I just needed to get my foot in the door before I tried to bust it open.

I understood. I was starting at the bottom rung again, and I was cool with that. I was ready to start that climb, whatever sacrifices it required.

I just hoped Maddux would understand.

I called Mic and told him, then asked him how I should break the news.

"Just tell him, Cody. He can take it. This whole thing's been such an amazing ride for him, he's not gonna be upset. I've always told him to keep his expectations low anyway. Look at how many fights he had to stay home and miss before the first walkout. He got through that. He can get through this."

Mic was right. Maddux took the news in stride. All he cared about was that I was making good on our pact. I was keeping up my end of the bargain. I was in the UFC now, and he fully expected that I'd make my way to the top.

"As long as I get to walk you down for the title fight, I'm good," he said.

"Believe me, when I get to that title fight, you'll be there," I said. "Ain't no one stopping that from happening."

"Right on," Maddux said.

It still bothered me that Maddux wouldn't be there, though. He and Mic had been in every locker room since my third pro fight, and it didn't feel right that they wouldn't be in Vegas for my UFC debut.

I still wasn't making much money—hardly anything, in fact. At my level, the purse for a UFC fight would only be about eight thousand dollars. All that time and effort and potential bodily harm for eight thousand bucks. I didn't even have health insurance. I couldn't afford it. I was covered by the organization if I got hurt in the ring, but if I hurt myself in training or anywhere else, any treatment I received came out of my own pocket.

I was sure that Mic and Stephani were living mostly paycheck to paycheck like the vast majority of people in this country, let alone in the 922. I knew they couldn't afford to fly their whole family to Vegas just after Christmas and New Year's Eve, and it killed me that I couldn't fly them out myself. It seemed unfair. I was really bummed out about it, and that affected my training. It just didn't feel right to leave any member of my team behind now that I was on my way to the top.

Well, call it a Christmas miracle or something, because I don't even know how Todd Meldrum found out about my dilemma. I certainly didn't mention it. But somehow he heard that Maddux wasn't coming to Vegas, and he thought it was awful. He thought the story of me and Maddux "saving each other" was the most inspiring part of this whole journey. So he stepped up and bought tickets to send Maddux and his whole family to Vegas for my fight.

To me, that was one more bit of proof that I was on the right path, and God was providing. Prayer. Support. It all went hand in hand.

When the news got back to me, I texted Todd: "Dude, I don't even know how to thank you."

He texted back: "Knowing that kid's face is gonna light up when he sees you knock out Brimage is all the thanks I need."

Todd didn't even really care about placing logos on my clothing anymore. He said he wasn't doing it for the advertising. He was doing it for me, and now he was doing it for Maddux. (That was a good thing, since it wouldn't be long before Reebok would buy out all the rights to UFC clothing sponsorship, so all of the little independent sponsors were about to disappear from UFC gear.)

"Just keep winning," Todd said.

How could I *not* keep winning?

"So are you going to be there?" I asked. Todd told me that he didn't like to fly, so he wasn't going to come.

"Come on!" I texted. "You can hang out and party with us."

"Nah. I'm gonna throw an event at the bar and watch the fight there. My son has said he'll be there. I'm all good!"

I was pretty sure that Todd had gone through some ups and downs with his son, who was eighteen now. I'd sent him over some gear for Todd to give to him, and apparently his son had thought that was cool. And now he was gonna go hang out with his dad to watch my fight.

So many people had been brought together in the course of this journey.

I felt more blessed every day.

⸻

Vegas was even more insane than I'd imagined. Driving down the Strip was like seeing the Golden Gate Bridge for the first time. It was way more impressive in person than it was on TV. There's just no way that cameras can capture how huge those buildings are and how bright the neon lights are and how crazy big the crowds are in those massive casinos. The MGM Grand is one of the biggest, and the Garden Arena, where the UFC fights are held, holds seventeen thousand people. Seventeen *thousand*.

Just walking through the halls and hanging out backstage at that arena in the days before the fight, I walked by more legendary faces from UFC past and present than I'd ever imagined I would see in a lifetime. It was wild.

I started to get a little nervous—not about the fight, but about everything else. All the other folks there seemed to know where they were going, what they were doing, and how to handle the TV cameras and the interviews and all of the press that we needed to do before the fight. I hadn't even brought any nice clothes to wear on camera. I didn't have a manager to tell me these things, except for Bob, and he'd never come close to fighting in an event of this size. I felt completely green and kind of lost.

I was so wound up about it all that I might have turned to alcohol or drugs to get me through that week if I hadn't had my faith to fall back on. But by now I knew that every obstacle, every doubt, every new challenge I faced was just part of the journey. Being nervous—that was God's way of reminding me that I was doing what I was supposed to be doing. I was growing. I was in the game. I was on the path.

I invited Maddux and his parents to come into my hotel room the day before the big fight, a couple of hours before weigh-ins. I needed to see them and hopefully find a way to ground myself, because as calm as I tried to be in the face of all that new pressure, I wasn't all that calm. I'd been dreaming of this my whole life, and I felt like everything had to be perfect.

The weigh-ins would be broadcast to UFC fans all over the world. This was a first impression and maybe a one-and-only shot. And I'd been so focused on getting to 5–0 and making it into the UFC that it hadn't occurred to me just how big a deal this first fight was. If I came in and lost, there was a chance I might never get another UFC fight. That happens sometimes. You lose that momentum and suddenly people look at you like you don't have what it takes, and you're finished.

I could feel everyone around me walking on eggshells. I'd bulked up a bit in the prior week and then had to go through an awful weight cut. So I was hungry—and grouchy.

"Maddux!" I said when they came into my hotel room. "It's good to see you, bud." That kid always put a smile on my face. Steph and Mic both hugged me, and it felt really good to have my whole team together. Everything felt right in the world—for about two minutes. Then I pulled out some of my clothes and realized that everything had gotten wrinkled from being stuffed in a suitcase all week.

"Sh-t. Sh-t! Where's the ironing board?"

"I'll do it," Steph said. "What do you have?" She found the ironing board and plugged the iron in and took over.

"Thank you," I said. "I'll freaking burn myself or something if I try to do it."

"No problem," she said. I saw her give Mic a funny look, and Mic just shrugged. I don't think they'd ever seen me so tense before.

I started tossing clothes her way without even thinking about it.

"Um, you sure you want me to iron your underwear?" she said, holding up a pair of my boxer briefs. Everyone laughed.

"Yeah, why not? I gotta look good, Steph. Why not look good all the way through?"

Uncle Bob came into the room and said hi to the Maples, and I took one look at him and got angry. "Aw, man, is that what you're wearing to the weigh-in?"

Bob was dressed in some wrinkly jeans and a T-shirt. "We're going on national TV!" I said.

"That's all I brought, man," he said. "I didn't know."

"Take 'em off, Bob," Steph said. "Toss 'em here. I'll iron 'em." So Bob took his jeans off right there in front of everybody and tossed them to Stephani.

"Anybody else?" Steph looked around.

"I think we're good," I told her. "I think we're good."

I was so glad to have my whole team around me. When the time came, I wanted us all to walk down to the weigh-in together. We did, and everything went fine. But I stayed pretty tense for the rest of that day and the next one, too, until finally it hit me: I was *there*. I was at the UFC. None of the small stuff mattered. None of it. What mattered was what happened in that arena.

I was beginning to understand that this wasn't just a fight. This was a modern-day gladiator competition, and that arena was a modern-day Colosseum. For all the watching I'd done of the UFC, I had never really gotten that before.

I have always loved the movie *Gladiator*, with Russell Crowe. I want to go to Rome someday to see the real Colosseum. It's on my bucket list, just to see where the original gladiators fought. Because what we do in the octagon isn't all that different.

I think all of us fighters recognize that we could die in that arena. Something serious could happen. Even though there haven't been any deaths in the UFC—and the refs work hard to make sure rules are followed to reduce the risk—there have been deaths in smaller MMA events around the world. It's a brutal sport. But those guys back in ancient times were really fighting to their deaths—getting their heads cut off, fighting tigers, all kinds of crazy stuff.

There's a line from the movie *Gladiator* that always resonated with me. Russell Crowe's character, the gladiator Maximus, tells his troops, "Brothers, what we do in life . . . echoes in eternity." That's actually a famous quote from the Roman Emperor Marcus Aurelius. I've always believed it's true. And that line was in my head that night as I got ready to walk into the MGM Grand Garden Arena.

I could feel that crowd cheering for blood, win or lose. I felt like a real modern-day gladiator.

And I hoped that what I was about to create was an echo in eternity.

Boom-boom, clap! Boom-boom, clap! My walkout music started blaring through the speakers as the doors opened. The full-spectrum light show of the UFC event washed over me, and all I can say is there is nothing in the world that prepares you for the roar of a seventeen-thousand-person crowd.

It's one thing to be in an arena like that as a spectator. It's magic, and there's a reason so many people like to go to big concerts and events surrounded by that much human energy. But when you're the one all of those people are directing their energy toward—man, that is insane. You can feel the vibration of the crowd move through your whole body. And I know this sounds weird, but you can sort of feel the power and reach of the TV audience too—millions of people, all tuned in to *you*.

It was deep. It was deeper than anything I'd ever felt walking into a fight before.

Once I got inside the cage, I did my best to let the crowd and the lights and every distracting thought fade. There was only one thing that mattered at that point. If I wanted anything else to come true for me, for Maddux, for my family, and for my fighting family, I needed to do one thing: *win*.

Marcus Brimage was a veteran fighter, a solid fighter, and we mixed it up pretty evenly from the get-go. I'd expanded my repertoire of kicks, and I used them, but kicks were in his repertoire, too, and mine didn't seem to get me anywhere. I even slipped once after a kick and fell on my back. That might've been a fatal mistake if I hadn't been quick enough to pop back up before he had half a second to take advantage of it.

For some reason my boxing style was off that night. I'd been working hard with Uncle Bob, but maybe my nerves got the better of me or something. I didn't hold my usual stance, so I kept opening myself up. Luckily I noticed this before my opponent could take advantage of that.

All in all, my speed is what saved me in that match. I taunted Brimage a couple of times, dropping my arms down to my sides, just knowing that he wasn't quick enough to get me before I could raise them back up. I wanted to put on a good show out of respect to that crowd. So I danced around a little bit, too, just teasing the guy.

I saw a couple of opportunities to go for the knockout early on, but I didn't take them. I was finally in the UFC, and I wanted this fight to last. So I pulled back a little bit and got through the first round. I stayed at that level all the way through the second round too. It was now officially the longest fight I'd had in my pro career. That was a good milestone to mark, I figured.

"I know you see those opportunities he's giving you," Bob said at the break. "Take one."

He was right. It was time.

In the third round, Brimage repeated himself one too many times. He gave me the same openings I'd let pass by in the first two rounds, and this time I nailed him. I knocked him down once and went in for the kill, but somehow that fool got right back up. He went staggering backward, covering his head with his hands, but he was still on his feet. He should have stayed down.

I kicked for his head. I faked like I was going low and forced him to drop his hands, then clocked him with a right that sent him reeling back toward the cage. I followed up with a right, left, right, left, waited a beat to throw off the rhythm of his defense. And then *boom*! I crushed him with a big right that took him down once and for all. I knocked him out.

I won my UFC debut!

This time, when they offered me the chance to say a few words, knowing that I had an audience of seventeen thousand people in that room and hundreds of thousands, even millions, watching on TV and the Internet, I took the opportunity to publicly thank the one person I'd neglected to mention during my postfight interviews at my last few fights. My greatest inspiration. The reason I was there.

"This fight is dedicated to a little boy who's been battling leukemia. He's in the building tonight, and his name is Maddux Maple," I said.

The crowd applauded.

"Three and a half years ago, I promised Maddux that I was gonna make it to the UFC and win, and he promised me that he was gonna beat leukemia. Tonight we both made good on our promises."

Now the audience went nuts. People were cheering and looking around, hoping they might catch a glimpse of the kid I was talking about. I wished so much that I could see Maddux's face at that moment. I wished he was right there in the octagon with me. I felt myself tearing up at the audience response and just imagining what it felt like for Maddux to feel the vibration of that applause all directed his way.

I would find out soon enough that Maddux felt it all. When I saw him after the fight, he was crying tears of joy. His whole family had apparently been bawling up in section 216 after I won. Maddux told me it had been the best day of his life. "Better than Disney!" he said.

Mic came up to me and gave me a big hug and said, "Cody, I can die happy now because I've seen everything. I've seen the lowest of lows, and now I've seen the highest of highs. I've never seen my son as happy as when he saw you win that fight."

I got a series of texts from Todd Meldrum later that night. When his eighteen-year-old son saw me make that dedication to Maddux from the ring, he went up to Todd and told him that supporting me and then sending Maddux and his family to that fight was the best thing he'd ever done in his life. He apparently had tears in his eyes, and he told Todd, "You're the best dad ever." (Just thinking about that tears me up!) Todd's son insisted that he fly Maddux and his family out to every single one of my fights from that day forward. And Todd agreed!

The press loved the story about me and Maddux too. I did a bunch of postfight TV and radio interviews where they asked me all about it. And over the course of the next couple of days, Chuck Mindenhall from MMAFighting. com pulled together a huge piece about the whole thing. He interviewed me for a long time and also spoke to Maddux and Mic. He wrote about my history in Ohio, Maddux's history, and how the two of us supported each other. And after that story hit the Web, we got calls from people all over wanting to know more about the tale of the fighter and the kid with cancer.

In the piece, Mic expanded on the same thoughts he had shared with me after the fight, and I was really touched by what he said: "You can't even . . . unless you had a kid go through it, I don't want to get all mushy, but there were a couple of times we thought we were going to lose him. . . . And to see him look at Cody, like we'd look at Michael Jordan back in the day, and to see him hang out with him in the room, and to watch the joy on Maddux's face, and watch him cry because he was so freaking happy that he won. I'll never forget that."

Mic also said, "I will do anything to get Cody any love at all because I owe him my world. He helped my son get through it, and I truly believe that. There's no doubt."

And Mic managed to mention one very important thing in that article. He said, "If the UFC ever allowed him to walk out with Cody, that would probably top—I don't know if it would top the first win—but that would be like a Make-a-Wish type of thing for Maddux."

Bingo! Mic had done my job for me without my even asking. Of course the UFC would let Maddux walk out with me next time. It was a great story. It was all true. And it had a happy ending, with hopefully more happy endings to come. How often does that happen in today's world?

Of course, that meant one other thing too. There would definitely be a next time.

After that night, Maddux and I were on everyone's radar.

TWENTY-TWO

I WAS ON MY WAY TO THE BIG TIME AND I NEEDED
to look the part. I remembered what Urijah had told me: "Don't worry about
money. The money will come." I decided to take his words to heart and threw
caution to the wind. Instead of stashing every penny I earned to go toward
rent, travel, and living expenses, I took a big chunk of my earnings from that
first UFC fight, walked into the Hugo Boss store right there in Vegas, and
bought myself a brand-new designer suit.

For this guy, there would be no more TV appearances looking anything but sharp. And if I had my way, there were going to be a lot more TV
appearances.

Everyone who was anyone on Team Alpha Male understood the power of
visualization. And if any of them hadn't paid attention to the pact I'd made
with Maddux, they changed their tune after I got back from Vegas. We all
came together on the vision quest to see Maddux walk me out to the title fight.
It wasn't just me who wanted it anymore. Faber wanted it, and my teammates
and coaches wanted it too. They all got that vision in their heads, and we all
got started on making that vision a reality.

I wound up having six full months to train for my next fight: UFC 189
on July 11, 2015. The headliner was a guy who was fast becoming a household
name, Conor McGregor, in a championship fight against Chad Mendes. But
my fight was against a guy named Henry Briones from Mexico. Henry, sometimes called Enrique, was an older guy, more than ten years older than me, and

he'd been fighting MMA since way back in 2007. But he'd just broken into the UFC that past November, and he'd won his first UFC fight by locking his opponent in a choke hold in the second round.

The powers that be at the UFC thought we looked like a pretty even match. I was pretty sure I'd be able to beat him, though. Coming off of that win against Brimage, I was confident I could beat anyone. I'd have happily taken on McGregor if they'd let me.

During this six-month training period, I started flying back and forth to Ohio now and then—to see Maddux and my family, of course, but also to give pep talks to little kids in my hometown. I had become a local celebrity of sorts, and I was excited to give back to the community. I brought groups of kids into the gym and taught them some wrestling, and I got up in front of classrooms full of junior high kids to try to inspire them.

I think kids really need stuff like that at a younger age. By the time they reach high school, it's already too late for some kids. But the junior high and elementary kids are hungering for someone to look up to, someone to tell them they have a shot of actually making it.

That's what I tried to do in my talks. I talked about dreams and goals, and those kids talked to me about how excited they were for my next fight. It was cool—not just to have so much support, but to look into the eyes of those kids and realize they were truly grateful to have me there. I was making a difference—and I wasn't that old yet!

I remembered what it was like. I'd been in those same classrooms just ten or twelve years earlier. I hadn't really had anyone to look up to in the fighting world back then, other than Uncle Bob and some of the older wrestlers at school. The fighters I saw on TV seemed so far away.

These kids? They now had me. Even if I never got one step further in the UFC, they were proud to get to spend time with me. I knew some of them who were growing up in that fighting culture of the 922 would pursue this dream. Even if it was just one of them, I was proud to think that I might have a positive influence on him or her.

I noticed on Twitter that a whole bunch of them tweeted to UFC president Dana White after I left the classroom. They all said they were gonna join the UFC some day, which I think was a pretty good indication that my talk with them was a big success.

I was really glad about that, because something about achieving my dream of making it to the UFC had made me want to try harder to be positive. To make a daily effort to stay upbeat in all aspects of my life, good times or bad, and to make things better for other people too.

I tried to share that message with those kids too. Focusing on positive things throughout my days became a challenge, a game to me almost. I wanted to see how far I could take it, whether it was helping the other fighters or giving of my time to a cause I believed in or even just being a nice person and holding the door for someone at my favorite coffee shop. Just simple things.

I already mentioned how crazy important it was to me when Maddux would send me a text to say "hi" or "I love you." There were times when those texts turned my whole day around and set me back on course. What if we all took the time to do that sort of stuff every day? I mean, seriously, is that too big a price to pay for all of the blessings that we have just being alive on this planet? With all of the blessings that had come into my life, I felt like it was more important than ever to live up to a higher standard.

Oddly enough, the older I got, the more I realized that my mom had been the one originally responsible for instilling ideas like that in my brain. She'd taught us manners and consideration as well as discipline and the grind. Even when Zach and I were tearing each other's hair out in the living room most nights, Mom had always expected us to be polite. She would tell us sometimes, "Oh, you know, Betty saw you guys at the store and wanted to compliment you on how well-mannered you were. That really makes me proud." Somehow in all of the chaos of her own life, Mom had found the time to give us those foundations.

A couple of months before my next fight, though, it got real hard for me to stay positive about anything.

I'd already flown back home to tell Maddux in person that he could definitely walk me out to my next fight at the MGM. We filmed that moment for a little "Road to the UFC" documentary piece, and Maddux was so pumped up about it, I thought he was gonna break something. "Hopefully not a bone!"

I said, and we laughed about just how tough his journey had been. I'm sure it felt good for him to laugh about it after all those years of having to take everything so seriously—kind of like it felt good for me to laugh about getting KO'd in my last amateur fight.

There's power in laughter.

Todd had already arranged for Maddux's whole family to fly out to Vegas again, this time for the entire week leading up to the big moment. Fight Week was a big deal in the UFC, and Maddux was pumped about getting to be there. The Maples were all pumped.

But right after that all got settled, I hit a snag that made me wonder if I was going to be able to fight at all. My back went out again, and this time it wasn't just muscles. It was a disc problem, the kind of injury that requires one of two things—either lots and lots of time and physical therapy, or surgery. I didn't have time or money or patience for either—and yet, there was no way I was gonna let Maddux down. There was no way I could cancel that fight. So I decided that, no matter what, I would grind through it and show up in Vegas with a smile.

In my mind I didn't have a choice. I *had* to fight. But how could I fight with a back that kept locking up, shooting pain down my legs that was so severe I couldn't even train? There were days on end when I couldn't get out of bed. It was all I could do just to stay in shape. Four weeks out from the fight, I could barely walk.

I went to see a chiropractor who specialized in deep-tissue work, with the aim of working out the tissue damage around where this disc injury was inflamed. That helped a lot. Then I got into the float tank and the hyperbaric chamber again and tried to relax and focus it away. That helped some too. But the basic issue was still there.

I still didn't have any health insurance. Any treatment I tried was all on me and my supporters. And it wasn't easy to be worried about money on top of being worried that this injury could take me out of the game.

As Fight Week approached, I got downright terrified. I was worried about all of the lost training days I'd suffered. I was scared that I might go in there and make my back worse.

Then the news got worse. Two weeks before the fight, Mic called me to let me know that Maddux was in the hospital getting some tests. He'd gotten real sick, and he'd fallen. His legs were weak again. The doctors were worried that the cancer might be back.

"No!" I said.

Now, on top of worrying about my back, I found myself worrying every second of the day about Maddux. Staying positive at that point was a definite challenge—one I met better on some days than others.

Thankfully that last fear only lasted a few days. All of Maddux's tests came back clear. But there was still something up with his legs. He had to climb back into his wheelchair just to get around.

"That's all right," I told him. "I'll wheel you out to the octagon. It'll be awesome! Don't worry about a thing, okay?"

I could have used that pep talk myself, because there were days when I felt like I ought to be in a wheelchair too.

All of those big worries spilled over to the smaller but significant worry that I simply wouldn't be fighting at the top of my game. In order to fulfill my pact with Maddux, I needed to make a straight line of nonstop victories all the way to the title. I was proud of my undefeated pro record, and I wanted to keep it that way. I also didn't want to get knocked down to the bottom rung of the ladder again. I didn't want this climb to the championship to take years and years. I didn't think I had the patience for that. Somehow, I felt like I'd skipped up a few steps through all the press attention Maddux and I had received. That would be impossible to replicate if I lost and had to start over.

I was so worried about it that I sought out training at a couple of other gyms in my last few weeks of fight camp. I needed to find a strategy to defeat Briones without killing myself, and having some additional input was just what I needed. Urijah understood. He knew I was completely loyal and that I'd be back no matter where I went to find help.

Once I was back in the fold, though, Urijah sat me down for a little talk.

"Dude!" he said to me just before we left for Vegas. "You worry too much. You're going on and on about, 'I feel like this hasn't been right and that hasn't been right.' Cody," he said, "you need to go in there thinking of it like this. If this guy you're about to face in the cage were to come up and slap your girlfriend on the ass right in front of you and then grab your drink out of your hand and take a sip of it, would you think about what your 'preparation' was like and whether it was perfect or whatnot? Would you worry about your back hurting? Or would you pummel the guy?"

"I'd pummel the guy," I said.

"Right! There's no way in hell this guy is going to beat you up. That's all you got to worry about, so don't worry about the little preparations and all these little things that are wrong."

A spinal injury isn't exactly a little thing, I thought. But I saw what Urijah was saying. I got the message.

"Just don't worry about it," he reminded me again when we hit the ground in Vegas. "How long have you been wrestling? How long have you been fighting? You've been doing this your whole life, dude. Whether the conditions are perfect or not perfect, this guy is going to come in and try to beat you up. He's going to try to come in there and crush your dream. I'm sorry, but I know you. I've been in that cage with you on good days and bad, and there is no way he's going to do that!"

In other words, just as Uncle Bob had drilled into me before, the only person who could lose that fight was me. I needed to stop worrying and get out of my own head. But that wasn't easy. Sometimes I think the hardest thing we ever have to do in life is get out of our own way.

Having Maddux around for Fight Week was what helped me turn all that worry around. Just being in his presence grounded me and reminded me of why I was there. It was also just plain fun hanging out with him. The city was jam-packed that hot week after the Fourth of July weekend, and Maddux's wheelchair turned out to be a godsend. We used it like a brush hog and said "excuse me" as we mowed through the crowds so we could get where we needed to go. And I actually knew where to go and knew what to do this time, which made Fight Week much more enjoyable for all of us.

I didn't tell the Maples about my back, though. I didn't tell anyone who didn't already know what I'd been through up in Sacramento. We'd decided it was best to keep that problem out of the limelight.

I have to say I did a great job of masking any stiffness or pain. Maybe I learned that skill from Maddux. But inside? Inside I felt like screaming.

The night before the fight I thought long and hard about canceling. I kept thinking, *What if I get knocked out? What if my back gets hurt worse? That could ruin everything. All my dreams could go up in smoke.*

But that very night, the UFC aired the TV segment on Maddux's story. They wanted fans to watch out for him during his big debut walkout for the UFC, and the piece those producers put together was heart wrenching. They nailed it. They captured Maddux's personality and his strength. They captured Mic's and Stephani's strength too. They made my journey to the UFC sound absolutely epic.

By the time that piece ended, I had made up my mind about whether or not to walk into that arena the next day. My love for Maddux won out over every fear I had.

If I lost, I would deal with the consequences. If I hurt myself, I would chalk it up to experience and hopefully find a way to come back. I'd done it before. But if I canceled, Maddux would be crushed. I couldn't let that happen.

This is about him, I reminded myself. *Win or lose, he's gonna get his walk.*

So on July 11 Maddux walked me out to the octagon in front of seventeen thousand people. That little man was beaming. I got real emotional on the walkout, thinking of everything he'd been through and how big a moment this was for him. I had to hold back tears before I got in the cage, which was definitely a new thing for me.

Maddux was right there in the front row to see all three agonizing rounds of that "evenly matched" fight. What neither he nor anyone else realized was that the only reason it was even close to an even match was that my back completely locked up on me in the first round. My biggest foe was my injury, not my opponent.

I tried to take Briones out on the ground early, but it didn't work. That whole strategy, which I'd developed at another gym, didn't work out at all. So I changed gears and went back to my roots—to Uncle Bob's Numbers and the boxing basics he'd taught me. I stood tall and fought through the pain in my back, a pain that shot down through my legs and nearly sent me to the floor without Briones having to lay a finger on me. I fought through it all.

It was the first professional fight I wasn't able to win by knockout. But even in my compromised condition, even with all that pain, I won—by unanimous decision.

That kind of blew my mind as I made my way back to the locker room. I had just won my second fight in the UFC, and the only reason I even went through with that fight was Maddux Maple. He didn't *know* he was the reason. He had no idea what he had done for me. All he knew was that we had fulfilled yet another promise on our road to the championship, and the joy of that was written all over his face.

As I fell asleep that night, I realized that Urijah had been right. I needed to stop worrying, to trust my own skills as a fighter and also trust in the Lord. As long as I was fighting for Maddux, I knew I was on the right path.

The funny thing is that after that night, everyone knew the full extent of what Maddux and I had promised. I had gone on camera for that TV segment and said out loud, for the whole world to hear: "Maddux and I made a promise. I told him, 'I'm going to make it to the UFC, and I'm not going to stop until we climb that ladder and I become the UFC champ!'"

That bold claim of mine was out there now. It was public. That meant the whole world would be watching me that much closer—to see if I could pull off that miracle, or to watch me fail. It suddenly felt as if I'd made that promise not just to Maddux, but to everyone who'd ever had a dream.

There was no place to hide.

TWENTY-THREE

I CHATTED WITH MADDUX OFTEN. I VISITED HIM when I could. We sent each other snaps. And my life, for the most part, started to find a certain flow that I'd never experienced before.

My next fight wasn't scheduled until February of 2016, and I was glad. I needed that time to let my back heal. I wound up finding a fantastic chiropractor, Dr. Yong Kim, who specialized in something called "Active Release Technique" (ART). Knowing that I didn't have any health insurance, he was kind enough to work on me and some other guys in the gym for free.

Dr. Kim worked miracles. My back started to truly heal. And during the downtime of that recuperation, the rest of me seemed to heal too.

By the late fall, I started to feel like struggles in my life—the ups and downs, the highs and lows, the wins and the injuries—weren't quite so dramatic anymore. I was starting to feel a lot more peaceful, and that feeling was oddly a little uncomfortable. The only life I'd known for so long was a full-on roller-coaster ride. It's hard to step off that ride after so long without getting the sensation in your stomach that you're about to take another drop.

Instead, as we headed into the holiday season, I got a different sensation in my stomach. A good one.

I met someone really special.

When I say "met," I don't mean in person. That would be too old-school. I mean I met her inadvertently through Snapchat. I noticed her in the background on one of my friend Johnny Nunez's snaps one night, and I asked him about her. Turns out, she asked him about me too. I went on Instagram and checked her out, not knowing that she'd done the same.

Her name was Danny, and I asked Johnny to introduce us. Before I knew it, Danny and I exchanged phone numbers and started talking. We didn't meet in person because Danny lived in Las Vegas. I didn't have any money to fly out there, and I really needed to stay focused anyway. I needed to stay on the path.

So Danny and I just chatted, talked on the phone, and FaceTimed. That was it. For months. It was weird. We would send messages back and forth for hours or spread out our conversations over the course of days on end, and we never failed to make each other laugh.

From the day I got Danny's number, not a day went by that we didn't talk. Not one day. We never failed to cut through the BS and small talk, either. For some reason, even without meeting face-to-face, we started opening up about our backgrounds and some of the stuff we'd both been through as kids.

Danny was a survivor of some pretty rough stuff that was easily on par with anything I'd faced in my family or in my town—even with my dad's prison, my mom's struggles, and all my fighting. But Danny's struggles were clearly behind her now. She had emerged from all of that to turn into one of the most positive people I'd ever met. She always seemed to see the good side of things. Even when I had something bad to say about something that was going on in my life, she'd find something good about it. She didn't complain much about anything; instead, she spent time talking about spirituality and traveling and making the most out of life. *She is exactly the kind of person I want to be around*, I thought to myself.

Oh, and did I mentioned that Danny was beautiful? I'm talking *stunning*. And she was interesting. She had family in Thailand, and she spent a lot of time there. I found that fascinating. It was so far from the world I knew.

She also seemed really patient. She understood that I was in training, and she seemed to be okay with waiting to meet until after my fight. I almost broke down and borrowed the money to fly down and meet up with her before then. I felt like I couldn't wait! But I was just so broke, and I didn't want her to know that, and she was so cool about it all that she made me almost *want* to wait—just because it was the right thing to do. She wanted me to do well.

She wanted me to stay focused. She said that was way more important to her than rushing anything.

It's funny to think about, but take away the phones and replace our texts with pen and paper, and the fact that we corresponded for months without ever meeting in person sounds like something from a romance novel set in the 1800s. There was something really cool about it. In this day and age when people tend to hook up first and fall in love later, we got to know each other and really like each other before we ever laid eyes (or anything else) on each other.

That long-distance, phone-only relationship gave me one more reason to stay focused on preparing for a successful fight—because after that fight was over, I had a new goal to achieve. I had to find some way to get to Vegas and take Danny on a date.

My next fight, my third UFC fight, wasn't going to happen in Las Vegas. It was a UFC Fight Night at the Consol Energy Arena near my old stomping grounds in Pittsburgh, Pennsylvania. It was the first UFC fight that had the possibility of drawing a good-sized hometown crowd for me, and I was excited about that. It was an easy fight for Maddux and his family to get to, and he was more pumped than ever to be a part of my walkout crew so close to home. I was pumped up about that too.

My opponent, Augusto Mendes, was undefeated. He had a professional record of 5–0, the very same record I'd had when I got my first fight in the UFC. As fate would have it, this was going to be Mendes's very first UFC fight too. I loved that. I remembered how hungry I'd been for that first UFC win. I remembered how powerful that momentum and drive had been, knowing I had finally arrived.

But even though I had some sympathy for the guy, I wanted more than anything to stop him in his tracks. There was no way I was going to let any man steal my dream. Not now. Not after all I'd been through. Not after overcoming yet another injury, going through another recovery. And not with Maddux at my side.

Maddux was feeling good. He was out of the wheelchair and raring to go, but the logistics of having him walk out in that particular arena didn't fly this time around. He wasn't fazed by that. He was happy to sit in the stands with his mom and dad, in seats right next to Todd Meldrum and his son. I spent time with him before the fight, though, and I asked him once again which hand I should use to knock out my opponent. This time he picked my right.

Stepping out into that Pittsburgh arena full of fans felt like a homecoming. This wasn't one of my old fights where I had to sell tickets to try to pack the house. Those fans just showed up on their own. They knew who I was—and they were loud about it.

Bruce Buffer, the voice of the UFC, was there to announce that fight, and the louder the crowd got during my introduction, the more he seemed to milk it. I fist-bumped Buffer as he said my name.

Let me say that again: I fist-bumped Bruce Buffer.

Do you know how surreal that was? I had listened to that guy's voice on TV since I was in middle school. I had heard that voice in my head, calling out my name, ever since I started dreaming of winning a belt in the UFC. Now here he was doing it for real, in front of our crowd, in my third-ever fight for the UFC.

I had been scheduled to fight another fighter going into that night, but the guy got sick—with dengue fever, of all things. I was glad—not because the guy was sick, but because Mendes was a better opponent for me. He had a black belt in jiu-jitsu and a different fighting style than anyone I'd gone up against in my previous UFC fights. I loved the new challenges the whole thing presented, from adjusting to an unexpected style to fighting at a different weight. (I had bulked up last minute and weighed in at 140.5 just to pull this off against his 142.) It was all good! I embraced those changes, and I focused on the goal.

Within the first thirty seconds of the fight, I landed a kick to Mendes's stomach and hard left to his head. I thought it was gonna be over really quick. But Mendes was quick himself, and he dodged a bunch of my strikes. I kicked his left leg repeatedly, and I threw him against the cage at one point, but I was careful not to let him take me down to the ground. I had a feeling, knowing what little I did about his history, that he might be stronger on the ground than he was standing up. So I kept him moving and waited for my moment.

At 4:41 I saw my spot. I hit him with an old Numbers combo: a light right, a quick hook left to draw his attention, and then—*boom!*—a big right to the center of his face for the knockout. He didn't see it coming, and he went down hard. The ref stepped in to call the fight before I landed a second hammer fist to Mendes's head.

A lot of people complained afterward that the ref called it too early. But I knew that Mendes wasn't getting back up, and so did he. If anything, that ref saved him from a more serious injury.

Once the referee called it, I jumped up to the top of the cage and let the roar of the crowd wash over me. And I looked out at an overjoyed Maddux as the roar washed over him too.

As I headed back to the locker room that night, I noticed Mic and Steph were wearing the orange "Madd About Maddux" shirts they'd printed for our very first fight together. It was hard to believe how much time had passed so quickly between then and now. I had lost that amateur bout to Jerrell Hodge on February 18, 2012. And I beat Mendes on February 21, almost exactly four years later.

Four years is the same amount of time someone typically spends in high school or college. And maybe there's something magic about that four-year time span during that formative time of our lives. Because the way I was living my life now, I felt like I'd graduated. And winning that fight after coming off of my back injury felt like a commencement ceremony.

I looked at Maddux that night and really noticed for the first time just how much he'd grown up since I first met him. He was taller now. He didn't have as much of a baby face. He still had the blue eyes of a warrior, but they were now staring out from a nine-year-old's face. He was growing up with all of that wisdom behind him and inside him already, and he was a really good kid. He was good to his sister, good to his parents, never hurt anyone, never *wanted* to hurt anyone. Always smiling. Always ready to help. Always enthusiastic. He seemed to be all of the things that his parents said he'd been as a little kid before the cancer came. He seemed happy just to be alive.

I was proud to know him and have him in my life.

"We're one step closer," I told him.

"Yeah, we are. You were awesome!" he said. "We're going all the way!"

I believed him. Any remaining doubts I'd had about myself disappeared that night. Maddux had helped me believe that any fight could be won in this life. And the work I'd done on my mind and body in the last seven months had done wonders. I was finally in a better place in my life, and that place felt really good.

I was now 3–0 in the UFC, still undefeated as a pro fighter. The top brass at the UFC had been watching my climb, and after this one, they decided I was ready for the big show.

It was just a few days later that I confirmed my next UFC fight. They were putting me up against Thomas Almeida, a powerful fighter from São Paulo, Brazil, with a 4–0 record in the UFC. He was undefeated, just like me. He was twenty-four, just like me. The main difference between us was that I was still an unranked fighter, while he was number seven in the world.

My pro record was impressive: 9–0 since I started. His pro record was *insane*: 21–0. Which meant that this guy had a lot more fight experience than me and that I was coming in as a serious underdog. And this fight wasn't going to be buried a few slots down the card. Almeida and I were the headliners!

"UFC Fight Night 88: Almeida vs. Garbrandt" was set for May 29, 2016—Memorial Day weekend—at the Mandalay Bay Events Center in Las Vegas.

This was gonna be huge.

And here's the really wild thing. The UFC asked me to fly to Vegas "right away" to make the announcement and do some press about the fight.

I'd gone and gotten myself all worried about how I was going to pull together the money and time I needed to fly myself to Vegas to finally take Danny on a date. And once again, a certain Somebody upstairs seemed to keep reminding me that I really shouldn't worry about anything. Ever.

When you're on the right path, God provides.

I picked up my phone and called Danny. "Hey, wanna go to dinner with me?"

"What?" she said. "When?"

"How about tomorrow night?"

"For real? You're coming to town?"

"I am," I said. "And I can't wait to see you."

"Me, either!"

"So is that a yes?" I asked.

"Yes!"

I flew out to Vegas the next morning and for the whole flight I could barely sit still. My stomach kept doing flips. Right after I landed, I made a reservation at STK, a high-end, ultramodern steak house in the heart of everything that crazy town has to offer, right on the Vegas Strip.

I was a little worried that I might not have enough money to pay the bill if we ordered too much. That place was pricey. I had a plan all worked out in my head to eat really light and drink nothing but water if I needed to. I could blame it on my fight diet, and I was pretty sure she wouldn't think twice about it. But after I did my press tour to announce the biggest fight of my career, the UFC paid me a stipend for my time. So I went to the restaurant feeling flush with cash.

I decided to wear my one pair of Hugo Boss slacks from the suit I'd bought, along with the button-down shirt I'd bought to go with that suit. They were the only nice clothes I owned, and I'd already worn them for press day. But I remembered from an earlier conversation that Danny liked getting dressed up, so I decided to keep them on for dinner.

When she picked me up at the Palace Station Hotel, my heart started racing. I could barely catch my breath. Laying eyes on her in person for the first time, I'm pretty sure I went flush in the face.

She was even more beautiful than her Instagram account let on.

She looked fantastic, and I was glad I hadn't dressed down.

"Wow, you look amazing," I said.

"So do you," she said.

She gave me a hug, and I didn't want to let go.

It was just so strange to be on a first date, to have never laid eyes on each other, but to already have a really deep understanding and knowledge of each other. For some reason I was really nervous all the way to the restaurant, and even when they took us to our table I kept looking down, like I couldn't even look her in the eyes. She laughed at me and called me out on it too. "I'm sorry," I said. "I'm really nervous."

She was just so stunning, and I had never been to a nice dinner in a place like that—certainly not in Las Vegas. I didn't know what to order. I didn't know how to act. But she reached across the table and took my hand, and I swear the whole city just melted into the background. Suddenly all of the noise and the people and my nerves went away.

"Hey," she said. "I'm nervous too."

"Maybe that's a good thing," I said.

We had spent so much time on the phone talking about our journeys in life and all the lessons we'd learned, I was pretty sure she understood what I meant by that.

She let out a little laugh. "Yeah. Maybe it is."

It didn't take long before we were talking and laughing just like we did on the phone. The food was incredible. Sitting there enjoying her company in person with the lights and loudness of Vegas all around us started to feel as comfortable as going to dinner with friends at the Dennison Yard. By the end of dinner, I couldn't take my eyes off her.

From that night on, Danny and I were together. We've been together ever since. Just like that, another part of my vision had come together—this time long before I ever expected it would.

It was hard to go back to Sacramento the next day, but I had to. My fight with Almeida, my first ever headliner for the UFC, was only three months away. The world would be watching, and I needed to be in the best shape of my life. I needed to do the work. I needed to "take my medicine."

Danny's encouragement became my fuel. We spoke on the phone every morning when I woke up. We spoke during the day when I was on break. We spoke at night before we went to bed. I told her all about the workouts I was doing, and she'd say things like, "Wow, you work so hard. You're doing so good. I'm so proud."

I'd never had anyone say those kinds of things to me on a daily basis. I definitely had never connected so deeply to anyone I'd dated. Just the sound of Danny's voice became a whole new motivation for me. It's as if she was the last piece of the puzzle, the one piece that I didn't even realize I needed, to make my life complete.

The only thing that frustrated me about our relationship was that I couldn't be with her in person. The distance was hard, and the lack of money made it harder. I didn't understand how I could still be this broke when I'd climbed so high.

Urijah kept insisting, "The money will come. Just be patient, dude!"

But my desire to spend time with Danny broke some of that patience down, for sure. I tried to trust that this was how it was supposed to be. After all, I was in training camp. I needed to stay focused.

It was just hard because Danny and I were crazy about each other. Even though we'd barely spent any time together in person, we both felt like we were meant to be together.

I couldn't wait to see her again.

I suppose in some ways that motivated me too. I knew there would be bonus money if I won a headlining event. I didn't know how much it would be, but anything would help.

So in addition to wanting to win that next fight for Maddux, who would once again be walking me into the arena, and in addition to wanting to win that fight in order to take the next step toward my shot at the title, I now had an added incentive: I could not wait to win that fight just so I could spend some time with my girlfriend.

TWENTY-FOUR

GOING INTO FIGHT WEEK FOR MY HEADLINING fight against Thomas Almeida, I had fifty-six dollars in my bank account.

That was all the money I had in the world.

Yet once again, God provided me with everything I needed. All my meals and lodging in Vegas were paid for by the UFC, and Danny was close by. She was able to come spend time with me at the hotel, to watch me work out and to meet my team. She met Maddux and Mic and Steph and Makyah. She met my brother, Zach, and my Uncle Bob. She met Urijah and some of the rest of the Alpha Male gang. She even met my mom—all in one week!

Danny got thrown right into the middle of my crazy life and huge extended family, and she somehow took it all in stride. She witnessed all of the hype around the fight, with the media and the fans, and she didn't seem fazed by it. She stood by and smiled while I posed for photos and answered questions from fans and interviewers. She came to my weigh-in. She hung out and laughed with everyone I knew. They all liked her, and I think they all saw how much I liked her, and that was cool.

The only thing that worried her was the fact that I actually had to fight that weekend. And that was a pretty big worry to have, given my chosen career. She got real nervous that I might get hurt. I reassured her the best I could, and I insisted there was nothing to worry about, but it was Maddux who seemed to come closest to putting her at ease. "No," he said. "You don't understand. Cody's the best. He's going to be world champion. He's not going to get hurt. It's not happening."

"Okay, kiddo," she said. "If you say so!"

Maddux had something funny happen when they first arrived in town. The family was walking across the casino floor on the way to their hotel room when a blackjack dealer, a perfect stranger, yelled out, "Hey, you're Maddux. Good to see you, kid!" and gave him a big thumbs-up.

"Dude, you're famous now!" I told Maddux.

"That's weird!" he said.

But I wasn't exaggerating. Maddux was famous, and he was the very reason I was standing where I was at that moment.

Danny thought it was so cool to finally get to talk to him after all I'd said about him over the phone. "You were right," she said. "His voice, his whole demeanor—he's just so sweet and kind."

Once again, I went into that fight feeling like I couldn't lose. I *wouldn't* lose, because I couldn't let Maddux down.

Plus, on top of everything else I had in my favor going into that fight, I kept thinking, *There is just no way some Brazilian guy is going to come into this town and beat up an American on Memorial Day weekend*. I felt like I was carrying the sacrifices of American soldiers' lives on my shoulders as Maddux and I walked out to that cage.

It was time for me to send another echo into eternity, and I did, right out of the gate. Almeida had more reach than me. Significantly more reach—nearly four and a half inches. A lot of people thought that might be my undoing. But I quickly learned I didn't need to be that worried.

I started out with a couple of big kicks, wanting to keep my distance, but I quickly realized that his boxing style had all sorts of openings. If I got in close, I was sure I could knock him out, so that's exactly what I did. I hurt him with a couple of strikes to the head early on, and I don't think the guy ever recovered. He stood strong. He even tagged me a couple of times. But halfway through the round, I saw my openings, and I took them. He tried to hit back, and the fight turned into a straight-up slugfest.

From the outside, it looked like an old-school boxing match. And I don't think boxing was his game. I pounded him so hard that the ref jumped in and physically threw me off to stop the fight.

I went scrambling up the cage like a monkey and roared to that crowd from the highest perch I'd ever reached in my life. I'd toppled the number-seven bantamweight fighter in the world, in the first round, when I wasn't even ranked!

During my postfight interview I gave Almeida credit for being the great fighter he was. But I also set my sights higher. I knew this fight was huge, and I knew that it wouldn't take much more for me to convince the UFC to give me a shot at the championship belt. So I used that opportunity to call out the fighter at the very top of my division. The current belt holder. A longtime rival of Urijah Faber. The guy I was now gunning for.

I said, with full confidence, "I'm the hardest hitter in the division. I'll knock anybody out in the division—Dominick Cruz, whoever. I'm gonna be the champion. Maddux Maple's right over here. I told him I was gonna give him the belt years ago, so my goal is to bring the world champion back to the 922!"

Last, I took a moment to dedicate my win to the men and women who fight for our country. I draped myself in the American flag, and I turned to celebrate with my team. I looked down at Maddux in the front row, dressed in a Garbrandt T-shirt, his newly grown hair peeking out from beneath a Garbrandt baseball cap, and I knew we were closer than ever to fulfilling our destiny.

~~~

I wound up getting called into Dana White's office the next morning. In all of my fights, I'd never had the opportunity to meet the president of UFC. But after that performance I'd given, he was the one who wanted to meet *me*.

I took Danny with me. I didn't have a manager at that point, but she was my partner now, and I wanted her there for everything. I felt like she had given me the extra support I needed to win that fight. And I wanted everyone to know that wherever I went, she was welcome too.

So we walked in, and I said, "What's up, man?" I shook Dana's hand and felt like one more part of my vision was coming true.

"How does it feel?" he asked.

And I was like, "Why? Are you guys surprised that I did that? I wasn't."

I think they thought I was hella cocky. But it didn't feel cocky to me. I had envisioned winning that fight, and I had envisioned winning the belt. I had achieved everything I'd achieved so far by the grace of God and because of Maddux, because of Zach, because of Mom and Uncle Bob, and because of the support of the incredible team of coaches and partners who were right there with me in spirit even when they weren't with me in person.

But maybe I didn't realize the magnitude of that fight and what it really meant. I think these guys were planning on elevating whoever won that fight in a big way, really blowing them up within the organization. Because after I left that office, my career did blow up—big time. Suddenly, my name was everywhere. I had new sponsorship opportunities coming out of nowhere. The story of me and Maddux seemed to gain more and more attention. Even Uncle Bob started gaining more attention, as other fighters up and down the UFC asked about my striking techniques. Soon they were reaching out to him about training possibilities.

"Yo," I told him. "Don't give away all our secrets." But I knew he wasn't going anywhere. The only other people he would share his techniques with were members of Team Alpha Male.

Oh, and one more thing came out of that meeting with Dana White: a nice bonus check. It wasn't enough to retire on or anything. It wasn't the kind of money some people might imagine a UFC fighter makes. But it was the biggest check I'd ever seen, and it was enough to let me put my day-to-day worries about money aside for a good long time.

I was on my way. That last frustrating missing part, the money I'd done without for this entire journey, was finally starting to roll in.

Suddenly my life went into hyperdrive. The UFC set my next fight for August 20, less than three months down the road. They put me up against Takeya Mizugaki, a veteran fighter who'd been with the UFC since 2011— back when I was still an amateur. Back when I first heard about Maddux.

This guy had an extensive win record, but I was more interested in his losses. Way back before he joined the UFC, he'd lost a fight to Urijah Faber. I hoped I'd be able to gain some insight on that firsthand from Urijah himself.

And in 2014, he'd lost a fight to Dominick Cruz, the current champion, Urijah's rival, and the guy I was now gunning for.

The reason they gave me this fight seemed clear: if I could beat Mizugaki, I would get my shot at the title. If I could beat Mizugaki, the UFC would let me fight Dominick Cruz for the belt.

I FaceTimed Maddux to share the news.

"This is it," I told him. "This is my shot. If I win this, you'll be walking me out for the title match next."

"*When* you win this," Maddux quickly corrected me, "I'll be walking you out to *win* the title match."

Man, I loved that kid!

Maddux was doing great. He was doing good in school, and he hadn't suffered any major health setbacks. Occasionally he would trip and fall because of his still-weak legs, and sometimes a bruise would take a long time to heal, but otherwise he was pretty much living the normal life of a nine-year-old boy. He played outside. He hung out with friends. He could run around on the playground. His hair was back. His doctors removed the port in his chest, leaving nothing but a small scar as the only physical indication that he'd ever been knocking on death's door.

Maddux's victory was real. It made me so happy every time I talked to him. He was the very definition of how to conquer. The warrior after the war.

On August 20, when we circled up in the locker room for our prefight prayer, I felt as good as I'd ever felt. No. I felt better than I'd ever felt. I was ranked now—number eight in the world. And I had everyone I loved either in those stands or in this room with me.

I asked Maddux which hand I should knock Mizugaki out with, and he said, "Your right." So I walked into that cage, and just forty seconds into the first round, I clocked him with a hard right. He went down, but he didn't stay down, so I hit him with a right again as he tried to stand up. He staggered back and looked like he was going to try to get up again, and since the ref didn't step in I let loose a series of lefts and one more right just to drive my point home.

The ref called it at forty-eight seconds. Another TKO in the first round.

I'd said that no man could stop me, and I meant it.

Now another battle had been won. The end was in sight.

When I came out of the cage, I kissed Danny. I hugged Maddux. I surrounded myself in the love of my whole team.

These people, these relationships, these angels, all mattered. Todd Meldrum. Uncle Bob, going way back when I was a kid. My mom. Zach! The one who kept me going, who introduced me to Maddux Maple, who changed my life. Urijah Faber, who inspired me long before I ever met him. And now Danny, who I planned to always have in my life. I recognized that these people and countless others had shown up just when I needed them—sometimes when I wasn't looking for them and didn't even know I needed them—and changed my life for the better.

They showed up. I saw them. I let them in. We connected. And that made all the difference.

It hadn't even been a year since I first started chatting with Danny, and she'd seen me rise from a mostly broke unranked fighter to *this*. Maddux and I had made it.

We were going for the belt. I was about to get my shot at Dominick Cruz.

TWENTY-FIVE

JUST FIVE DAYS LATER, ON AUGUST 25, 2016, Maddux celebrated another milestone: his first year with no chemo and his second year of remission. Just three more to go until he won the ultimate battle and got himself declared "cancer free."

As far as I was concerned, that kid was a bigger champion and a bigger inspiration than I could ever be. But still, I could not wait to become UFC champion for him.

The date was set. The wheels were in motion.

On December 30, 2016, I would climb into the cage at UFC 207, at the center of the twenty-thousand-seat T-Mobile Arena in Las Vegas to take my shot at the UFC Bantamweight Championship belt that was currently held by Dominick Cruz.

To put the scope of this into perspective, Dominick Cruz wasn't just the champion. He was the guy who'd stolen the bantamweight title away from Team Alpha Male. (One of my teammates and sometime sparring partner at Ultimate Fitness had held that title before defecting to another gym.) I wanted to steal it back—not only to avenge my team, but to settle the longstanding rivalry between Cruz and my main man, Urijah Faber.

Way back when they were first starting out as professional fighters, Faber had beaten Cruz in his very first match. That win had started a bitter feud that never ended. In 2011 the two had finally had a rematch, and Cruz had beaten Faber in a highly contested decision. Faber had dropped Cruz multiple times in that matchup, and a lot of people over the years had said that he absolutely should have won that fight. Faber certainly thought so. He'd never really gotten over the loss.

In June of 2016, I'd been there acting as a part of Faber's coaching team when Faber got another shot at taking the belt from Cruz, and I'd been devastated when Cruz knocked him down not once, but twice. The match had gone right to the end, and the judges had called it in Cruz's favor.

It was not the way Urijah wanted to go out—that's for sure. But he was getting ready to retire, and he knew he wouldn't get another shot at Cruz. So the way he saw it, I was now his best hope at getting some sort of payback.

Faber was the one who put the idea in the heads of the UFC powers that be. He told them, "My boy Cody Garbrandt hits a lot harder than Cruz. Why don't you give him a shot?"

My Uncle Bob teased him about it. "Yeah, yeah," he said. "Cody will go beat up that bully for you, Faber."

All joking aside, though, I was more than willing to do anything I could to avenge Faber. He'd been my hero for a long time, and now he had become my friend and mentor. I was more than ready to take on Cruz and, in the process, to win myself a championship.

Not long after the fight was confirmed, I spent some time in the float tank. It wasn't for my back or anything else at that point, since my body was doing what I needed it to do. It was more for my mind. Floating there in complete isolation for an hour is like getting eight hours of sleep.

The sensory deprivation does weird things to your mind too. There were times when I would almost hallucinate in there. And in one of my sessions after my fight with Cruz was announced, I had a vision in the tank and saw myself hit him with a hard right. I saw myself knock him out.

I hoped that vision was true—for me, for Urijah, and for Maddux.

It was hard for me to keep any sort of perspective on everything that was happening in my life. It all seemed so wild to me. When Fight Week came around, the level of media attention was beyond anything I'd ever imagined. The whole city of Vegas seemed amped up. The weigh-in was insane.

Cruz kept bouncing up and down, faking like he was going to come after me. Like he was putting on a show. He was like, "Come on, buddy," with one of his managers standing there pretending to hold him back. I wasn't pretending. I stuck my jaw out, like, "Dude, come on. Hit me." I would've loved to have gotten into it for real with that guy.

What he didn't realize is that I wasn't playing. Instead, I was taking advantage of that moment to study the way he moved. I noted the way his shoulder muscle twitched before he swung his arm out. It was a dead giveaway, and I would use that against him in the cage. It felt great. There I was standing face-to-face with one of the best fighters, pound-for-pound, in the history of my sport, knowing that I now had an edge on him.

Maddux was there the whole time, of course, just eating it all up, and Danny was right by my side, supporting me through the whole thing. None of the insanity of the prefight buildup fazed me because I had my team, I had my people, I had my family, and I had my faith that nothing could go wrong because everything was in God's hands. I was on the right path.

The only thing I had a hard time with during Fight Week was Uncle Bob. The man just kept crying, saying, "You're gonna be the champion. You're really gonna do it," and then he'd just lose it. It happened over and over again. Here was this ex-con, this hardened fighter, and it was like his whole life's meaning was getting played out through this moment. He was just overwhelmed by it.

I felt for the guy. I knew how much he cared about me, and I couldn't have been happier that he was happy. What greater gift is there than to make someone in your family feel proud and happy?

I knew my mom was proud and happy too. At one point Urijah asked her, "Are you nervous?" and she said, "No." This was the woman who wouldn't allow us to box for years because she thought we would wind up bashing our heads in, and now she just wasn't worried. She was confident that I was going to win and that I wasn't going to get hurt. I guess she figured if I hadn't broken my skull in by then, it probably wasn't going to happen.

The night before the fight, in the quiet of our hotel room, I thanked Danny for being there for me through all of it. I thanked her for handling everything she'd been thrown into, and I asked her, honestly, how in the heck she did it. Because I didn't think I could have handled all of that without the practice of building up to it over multiple fights at all different levels.

"I don't know," she said. "I just love you."

I knew that night that I wanted to marry her.

Things were so crazy at the arena that fight night that my entourage was limited. I was allowed to have Maddux with me, but I wasn't allowed to let Mic come in. We had to be in the locker room really early, so that meant Maddux and everyone else had to hang out for a good three hours before my actual fight time.

We all got a little punchy back there. We were goofing around and dancing and stuff. I was in a really good mood. We'd all been through this routine so many times now that we didn't stress over anything. I looked at Maddux at one point in that locker room, and once again, I was blown away by just how much he'd grown up. He had changed so much. And so had I. I didn't look that different on the outside, other than the fact that I'd added some more tattoos along the way and maybe gotten in better shape. But the interior changes I'd made, the maturing I'd done, the way I'd developed as a man—all that was huge.

I realized in that moment that I couldn't even remember what Maddux looked like back when this all started. It bothered me. The journey we'd taken together was so important to me, and I suddenly felt like I needed a visual reminder of just how far we both had come. So a little after nine that night, I sent a text to Mic. I knew he was up in the stands watching the early bouts and waiting anxiously to see his son walk into that arena.

"Send me a picture of Maddux in bed, fighting for his life, please," I wrote. "I need to see it. I love this kid so much."

A few minutes went by, and Mic came through. He sent me four photos of Maddux back when he first went into the hospital. He was so small! And he looked so fragile, so helpless lying there in that hospital bed.

One of those photos Mic sent was the exact photo I remembered seeing the first time Zach told me about Maddux. The one I'd seen on Facebook that caught me off guard. The one I'd stared at early on, when I decided I wanted, even needed, to do something to help this kid—as if helping him was something I was supposed to do.

It wasn't an overwhelming feeling. It wasn't some big revelation. I didn't hear the voice of God or anything dramatic like that. But on some level, especially now as I thought back on it, it truly did feel like receiving that call from Zach and seeing that first photo of Maddux in his hospital bed was some sort of a message from the big guy upstairs—maybe even a response to those prayers I'd sent up from my own hospital bed on the night I got stabbed.

I double-clicked that pic on my phone and zoomed in real close so I could see Maddux's eyes. Sure enough, he had that look in them that I remembered. That warrior look. That determined look of a fighter who was not going to lose, no matter what.

That look was exactly what I needed to see.

I thanked Mic for sending the pictures, and I turned my attention back to the Maddux I knew now. The fun kid in the locker room who always had a smile. My champion. My hero. My biggest fan.

As our fight time grew near, we circled up. Uncle Bob led us in prayer. We went through our usual routines. But just before we stepped into the hallway to make the long walk to the entrance to the arena, I bent down and looked Maddux in the eyes.

"No matter what happens out there, when this is all over, you know that we get to come back to our families and our lives, and that's what matters most, right?"

"Right," he said.

"Win or lose, we've already won," I said.

"Win or lose," Maddux echoed. "Except . . . I know you're gonna win."

I smiled.

"Which hand should I knock him out with?" I asked.

"Right hand. Definitely the right hand," Maddux said.

It was time.

"Let's do this!" I yelled, and my crew hollered back. I took Maddux's hand and started walking. But Uncle Bob wouldn't stop crying.

I stopped and grabbed the sides of his face. "Bob, get it together, man. I know this is emotional. But we still have to go out there and win this thing. I need you!"

After all the years of Bob calming me down before fights, I never expected we'd reverse roles on the night of my championship fight.

"Yup," he said. "Okay."

He finally pulled it together. So I grabbed Maddux's hand and started walking again, a little faster now.

We could hear the music through the walls. *Boom-boom, clap! Boom-boom, clap!*

Maddux had his focus on, and so did I. Laser focus.

As the doors opened, "We Will Rock You" blasted our ears. The crowd erupted. Everything was bigger than ever before. The lights were brighter, the cage that much farther away. We made that walk knowing that this was it. This was everything we'd dreamed of. This was the culmination of everything we'd promised each other.

We had arrived.

Climbing into that cage, soaking in the vibrations of the massive energy of that crowd, listening to Bruce Buffer call my name—all of it was perfect. I felt perfect. I had been here already in my mind.

I did my usual pacing like a lion in a cage, sizing up my opponent and looking for weakness. To me, in that moment, I swear that Dominick Cruz didn't have the old "Eye of the Tiger" like they talk about in *Rocky III*. I suppose he might have looked arrogant, but arrogant isn't the same as confident.

When we came in close for the instructions, I didn't smell hunger. I didn't even smell fear. I smelled nothing.

Cruz had won the belt before. He'd come back and won it again. It was a trophy to him. But for me that belt was a lifelong dream. That belt was a little kid's *life*. That belt was everything.

When the ref dropped his hand to fight, I knew I was there for bigger reasons than my own.

I was there for bigger reasons, period.

Cruz made a little juke step toward me. I threw a three-punch and then a left hook at him. He went back to the center of the cage and kinda bounced up and down, and I could see him shaking the cobwebs out. I'd hurt him already. I could see it clear as day. So I decided to toy with him.

I held up one finger and said out loud, "That one hurt ya!"

"No it didn't," he said. "No it didn't, you little b-tch."

His comeback was so weak, both verbally and physically, that a part of me thought, *This is going to be easy.*

I was in flow. Everything in my life was in flow.

I saw the twitch in his shoulder and anticipated his strikes. I felt like I could see almost everything he was going to do. He liked to bounce off the cage and explode out toward me, and I easily sidestepped it because he ran straight out every time. I was quicker than he was. He was older. He was a truly great fighter, but in this moment, to me, he seemed slow.

I had multiple opportunities to take him down in the first round, but I passed them all up. I was having too much fun. I wanted to enjoy every moment, so I egged him on. I taunted him. I'd taunted a few opponents in the past, but never in a mocking sort of way. I didn't even know where it all was coming from. I enjoyed landing strikes and saying, "Gotcha again!" then ducking his throws and saying, "Ah!"

I was positive that as long as I didn't get caught off guard, I couldn't lose. Then he caught me off guard.

He hit me with an odd left hook and cut my eyebrow. I started bleeding. It dripped down my face, and I enjoyed the taste of the blood. I liked the feel of it on my skin. It was hot, and it only got me more fired up.

As the fight progressed, I stuck my jaw out and said, "Come on!" I dared him to hit me, just as I'd done at the weigh-in. I wanted him to swing just so I could duck and counter and hurt him some more.

I even took a little time to dance in the ring. I was just full of absolute confidence, and I didn't want this moment to end. It had been such a long road to get there, such an incredible ride. I wanted to live out every moment of that fight to the fullest.

At one point I head-kicked him, and my knee cut his eyebrow. It was a huge gash that left him covered in blood. And once he was covered in blood, I heard the crowd chant, "Co-dy, Co-dy!"

It was unreal. I think that's when it started to set in that Dominick Cruz was the UFC champion, a longtime favorite, yet the crowd in that massive arena was on my side. The underdog's side.

Funny enough, that's when he caught me off guard again and hit me with his hardest shot so far. I actually welcomed it. I thought maybe he was going to bring an A game I hadn't seen yet. "Wow," I said. "Let's go!"

When he failed to follow up, I asked him, "Are you having fun yet?"

He touched the back of his hand to his bleeding eyebrow and then looked down at all the blood. I saw his pupils go real big. I just don't think he ever took me to be a serious challenger. Maybe there was something about me being trained under his old rival Urijah that made him think I was weak.

He was dead wrong.

He tried to come back a couple of times. He hit me with a naked jump knee that took the air out of me for a good fifteen or twenty seconds, which is a lifetime in the cage. He thought he'd hurt me, when all he did was take the wind out of me. I knew that as long as I slid back and gave myself a little break I'd be fine.

I'm surprised he didn't jump on me then. Normally when an opponent gets hurt, you jump on them. Maybe he was trying to make the match last too.

At that point, all of a sudden, the length of the match started to take a toll.

It was by far my longest and bloodiest fight ever. With ninety seconds left in the fifth round, my lungs were burning. My legs were tired, and I was pretty sure I'd torn the meniscus in my knee.

I suddenly flashed back and saw images in my mind that spread from my birth to that very moment. It's hard to explain. I flipped through pictures of everything I'd ever been through, almost like they say you do before you die, when your life flashes before your eyes. It felt like a chapter was ending. Like I was about to close the book.

I felt like I was outside of myself when I heard the clappers signaling ten seconds left in the fight.

This was it. The world championship. The culmination of everything Maddux and I had dreamed of. All I had to do was to hold on for 7, 6, 5, 4 . . . I threw my hands up and did a little dance move . . . 3, 2, 1!

When the horn blew, I jumped up on the side of the cage as if I had just knocked Dominick Cruz out.

I had gone the distance, and I knew what the outcome would be. I just knew.

The crowd went nuts the whole time we waited for the decision.

And then I heard the voice. That oh-so-familiar voice.

"And the winner is . . . Cody. *No Love.* Garbrandt!"

I raised my arms up and danced all over that octagon. The crowd was on its feet. The emotion of the moment washed over me, and I teared up.

Maddux and I, we hadn't just won the battle. We'd won the war. The war was over, and we'd won.

We'd won!

TWENTY-SIX

IF THAT WAS ALL THAT OCCURRED THAT NIGHT, IT would have been a pretty great ending. Two fighters covered in blood. The underdog defeating the champion. But somehow, hearing Bruce Buffer call out my name and feeling Dana White strap that big gold belt around my waist didn't feel like the ultimate moment of my life.

There's a reason for that, a very good reason. And the reason is that my championship fight wasn't about the fight itself. In fact, it wasn't even "my" fight. Of course it wasn't! That championship was about something maybe bigger than any champion fight in the UFC had ever been about.

As proud and happy as I was to fulfill my lifelong vision, I was way happier and more proud about what happened next.

When that fight was over, I pulled Maddux into the octagon. I put that now not-so-little boy in the center of the spotlight for all the world to see. And I gave that belt to him. It had been for him all along. Maddux had helped me to find the strength to change my life so that I was capable of winning that belt for him.

And that's what I told the crowd. I reminded the fans and told a whole new audience of people that Maddux and I had made a promise to each other and that now we had both won—because we both fulfilled our pact. I had beaten Dominick Cruz to win the championship. Maddux had beaten cancer. And those twenty thousand people cheered for the boy who had walked in beside me.

That is what that fight was all about, what the whole journey had been about—the fulfillment of the vision. The pact that the two of us had made with each other, and the pacts that we'd made along the way with ourselves, our families, and God.

The pact to live life to the fullest and to never give up. To live to fight. To fight to live. And as we do, to share a message of hope and love and caring and friendship. That's exactly what that fight will be remembered for as it echoes through eternity.

The press barely asked about the technical details of the fight itself after Maddux took the spotlight. All anyone wanted to know about was our story. I thought we had already made a lot of headlines and reached a lot of people before that moment, but that coverage was nothing in comparison to the number of media outlets and individuals we reached in the aftermath of that victory. Video of me giving that belt to Maddux went viral. People who didn't even watch or enjoy MMA fighting tuned in to that moment. That moment touched people's hearts—and that reaction, in return, touched ours.

I had told Maddux that whatever happened in that fight, win or lose, we'd go back to our families and life would be good. But I was wrong. After I gave Maddux that belt, the two of us wound up being pulled from media interview to media interview for nearly two straight hours. It was so crazy that I don't think we got the chance to reunite Maddux with his parents until sometime after one in the morning. And the whole time we went from interview to interview, Maddux carried that big heavy belt with a smile on his face.

He never put it down. Not once.

There were a few nice perks that came along with winning that belt. One of them was a big fat paycheck. But as with every other part of this journey, that paycheck wasn't all mine. I knew it belonged to a whole lot of other people.

I went to visit Uncle Bob and handed him a check. I told him it was back payment for all of the training he'd given me since I was a little kid. There was no amount of money in the world that could cover what he'd done for me and given to me—not just ring skills, but life skills too. And love.

"Cody, what are you talking about?" he said. "I didn't do any of that for money."

"I know you didn't, Bob. That's why you deserve this so much," I said. "I love you, man."

Bob started bawling again. And this time, I teared up right along with him.

I waited a little while to do something for Zach. I never would have made this journey at all if it weren't for him toughening me up and introducing me to Maddux and pushing me to keep going when I was just about ready to give it all up for a mining job. He had been my first real partner and teammate in life. So when his birthday came around, I bought him a brand-new Harley Davidson motorcycle—his dream bike, something he'd wanted since he was a little boy.

I won't list everyone else who got a present from me, but there is one other person who deserves a special shout-out.

My mom isn't a materialistic person, and I couldn't think for the life of me what kind of a present would be worthy of everything she'd given to me that helped me get to that championship. She had sacrificed so much in her life, and no gift I could think of seemed worthy.

But then it hit me. The gift I wanted to give her was one of the very things she sacrificed: shoes. I remembered that my mother had gone years between buying herself new pairs of shoes, just so she could have enough money to buy us the gear we needed and enroll us in the wrestling camps we wanted to attend. The woman had to come into my bedroom and take my wrestling shoes off at night, yet I couldn't remember her ever treating herself to even one nice pair of shoes.

I went out and bought my mom a whole bunch of brand-new shoes, enough to fill a whole closet. I wanted her to feel like the shoe princess of Uhrichsville. And I told her she could pretty much buy any shoes she wanted from that day forward. All she had to do was let me know, and her feet would never have to slip into an old pair of worn-out shoes again.

To be honest, I didn't have a ton of money left over after all my payment and gift giving was done. But I had more money than I'd had when I started, and that was more than enough for me. Because I was on the right path, and I was staying on that path. And I knew that God would provide as long as I stayed true to the journey.

In January the *Times-Reporter* ran a five-day special edition dedicated to our win. Each day the cover of the newspaper featured one part of a poster of a photo of me in the cage. When you collected all five and put them together, you wound up with a giant poster of me to hang on your wall.

I thought that was kind of ridiculous. I couldn't imagine that anyone from the 922 would want a big picture of me in their house. But apparently they sold a lot of papers, and I soon found out that my level of support back in my hometown was bigger than I ever would have expected.

On January 22, the town threw me and Maddux a big celebration. The two of us wound up in a parade, riding a float through town, waving to fans who gathered on sidewalks all over Dennison and Uhrichsville.

For a couple of weeks I'd been forced to keep the belt with me, carrying it around to press appearances while Maddux went back to school. But after the parade, we went back to the Maples' house so I could officially hand that championship belt back over to its rightful owner.

"You don't have to do this, Cody," Mic said, trying to dissuade me, just as he had many times before that moment finally came. "It's your belt. You won it."

"Mic, this belt is not mine," I reminded him. "It's Maddux's. It was all for him. It was all because of him. And that's the truth."

"Come on!" Maddux said, pulling Danny and me down the hall to see the "man cave" he and Mic had put together at the back of the house. Stepping into that room, I was stunned. The walls were all dedicated to the two of us. There were pictures we'd taken at various points along the way. He'd already put the five-part newspaper poster together and hung it on the wall. He had my first amateur belt all framed up nice. He had some pictures I'd signed for him and some promotional items and even the very first little white pair of kids' boxing gloves I'd given to him on the first day I finally met him in person. It was like stepping into a time capsule of our entire journey.

It brought tears to my eyes.

"Maddux, this is unbelievable," I said.

"I know, right? Can you believe we did all of this?"

"Want to know something else unbelievable?" Mic said. "Do you know what today is?"

"What do you mean?"

Steph jumped in to answer Mic's question. "It's January 22," she said. "Today is five years to the day from when you first came here to meet Maddux."

"No way," I said. "To the day?"

"To the day," Maddux said.

Danny looked at me, and I looked at her, and we both smiled as we shook our heads.

"Man," Mic said, "we are constantly reminded on this journey of how powerful the person upstairs is."

I held Danny's hand, listening to Maddux as he walked around the room proudly showing her pictures of everything we'd been through, taking in the laughter of Mic and Stephani as they took turns giving hugs to Makyah, and I thought, *Mic is exactly right. We are constantly reminded.* Constantly.

And in that room, standing there with those people, feeling the warmth of Danny's hand in mine and hearing the vibrancy in Maddux's voice, a sensation came over me that I had craved since I can't remember.

I felt peace.

AFTERWORD

WAY BACK IN WHAT MAY HAVE BEEN THE WORST moment in Stephani Maple's life, when the doctors drilled a bone-marrow biopsy needle into her son's leg to determine what type of cancer he had, they told her that Maddux would have no memory of that awful day.

They were right. Today, Maddux has no memory of that biopsy procedure at all. In fact, he has no memory of almost anything from those first terrible weeks in the hospital that were such torture for Mic and Steph. If it weren't for the pictures and stories they've shared with their son, plus the ones he's likely now reading in this book, Maddux would be happily oblivious to just how scary and awful things were when he was first diagnosed.

There are blessings to being young.

The memories he does have—the ones he will hold on to? They are of his mom and dad spending time with him and helping him to do the simplest things, from walking to brushing his teeth. To have two parents there, caring for you with all their hearts—I'm not sure a kid could have more important memories.

Then again, this kid was also going to be left with some of the wildest experiences any kid could imagine, including walking into the ring as part of the team for the crowning of the new bantamweight champion of the world.

My hope is that most of the tougher memories—the cancer memories, the chemo memories, the memories of the pain he so quietly endured—will fade into the background. Instead, I hope he'll remember the great times, the lessons, the strength he showed, the powerful friendships and overwhelming support he received from the great big community of giving people all around him who were so ready to lend a hand.

Memory has a way of doing that, doesn't it? The good stuff gets stronger, even bigger with time. The work it took all of us to get to those memories, the obstacles we overcame, the pain we endured—whether it's chemo side effects or a broken hand or even the pain of childbirth—they all fade to a place where they seem far less overwhelming than they did when we were actually going through them.

To me, that's a reason to hope. And so is the fact that if we're here, if we're still breathing, if we're still waking up in the morning, then we're still in the game. And as long as we're in the game, we should be thankful.

I'm happy to say that my whole extended family is still in the game right now.

My mom's in a good marriage.

My extended array of half-siblings and stepsiblings are all doing well.

Zach has a good job and is loving life.

My Uncle Bob is in high demand as a striking trainer these days.

Maddux and Makyah are both doing well in school.

Steph and Mic are back at the family business full time, caring for the perfect strangers who've been put in their care with pretty much the same sort of love and attention they give to their own kids.

As for my future plans? Professionally speaking, I think I've got a ways to go in the UFC. I went through a horrible back injury that kept me out of the octagon for nearly a year right after winning the belt. Then I lost the belt to former Team Alpha Male contender T. J. Dillashaw in an epic showdown at Madison Square Garden. But as you know by now, one fight will never define me.

For now, I'm enjoying the things that matter most—my family and the peace we earned. This journey we took wasn't just to reach the mountaintop of a UFC title. It was to reach the peak of beating Maddux's cancer. And on August 25, 2017, Maddux celebrated three full years in remission. As this book hits bookstores, he's only got a little more than a year and a half left to go to get to the official title of "cancer free."

It's just a matter of time.

I thank God for bringing Maddux into my life at just the right time for both of us—because there is no doubt that what we did for each other was nothing short of saving each other's lives. We gave each other the support and inspiration we needed to get through our battles, which we never could have fought quite as powerfully on our own. And because of that, we won life's greatest battle of all—the battle for survival, not only of our bodies, but of our souls and of our dreams.

Speaking of dreams, after winning the title I finally found just the right moment to ask Danny to marry me—at the top of a mountain in Sedona, Arizona, after taking a spiritual walk together that solidified everything we wanted out of life.

We got married in a private ceremony, completely out of the public eye. And a few months later, when I was right in the middle of working on this book, Danny surprised me with just about the greatest news I'd ever heard. She let me know that we're going to have a baby.

Everything, absolutely everything I ever wanted or imagined is coming true in ways that are far better than I ever envisioned.

God did that.

He did all of it.

The ups, the downs—every bit of it was exactly what needed to happen in order to get Maddux and me and everyone around us who we love and cherish to exactly the point where we are today.

And the best part is, I get it. I see it. And I'm thankful for all of it.

That's why I swear that every morning when I wake up for as long as I live, no matter what happens from here on out, I will continue to thank God. For everything.

STUDY GUIDE

USE THE FOLLOWING QUESTIONS TO FULLY ENGAGE the content in each chapter of *The Pact*. These questions can also serve as helpful discussion starters for reading the book as part of a group.

CHAPTER 1

1. What surprised you most in this chapter? Why?
2. How does Cody's upbringing compare and contrast with your own experiences as a child?
3. What's one of the biggest fights you've faced so far?

CHAPTER 2

1. Who have been some of the biggest positive role models in your life?
2. How would you describe what it means to live as a follower of God?
3. When was the first time you remember feeling legitimately proud of something you accomplished?

CHAPTER 3

1. What movies or other stories have helped you learn important life lessons?

2. When did you deal with disappointment for the first time? The loss of a dream?

3. Who has your back today when life doesn't go as you expected?

CHAPTER 4

1. What are some words you would use to describe the sport of Mixed Martial Arts (MMA)?

2. How did the important people in your life respond to your dreams and aspirations while you were growing up?

3. What are some "demons" that have threatened to derail your dreams and aspirations?

CHAPTER 5

1. When have you had to learn a big lesson the hard way?

2. How do you typically respond to criticism and critique?

3. What's a next step you can take this week on the way to achieving one of your goals?

CHAPTER 6

1. When you were growing up, who were some of your biggest heroes? Why?

2. Who gives you great feedback?

3. Where are you currently confronting a choice between doing what you want and doing what others want for you?

CHAPTER 7

1. What are some obstacles or patterns that get in the way of your ability to use your God-given talents?

2. What do you like best about Zach's advice to Cody on pages 56–57? Why?

3. How can you create more opportunities for the people you care about to speak truth into your life?

CHAPTER 8

1. What moments from your past might qualify as "rock bottom"?
2. How do you typically respond in a crisis?
3. Where are you currently considering giving up on a dream?

CHAPTER 9

1. What emotions do you experience when you read this chapter?
2. When have you felt drawn to someone you didn't know very well?
3. What steps can you take to prepare yourself today for crises that will happen in the future?

CHAPTER 10

1. How has your world been impacted by cancer?
2. Take another look at Maddux's bone-marrow procedure on pages 70–71. How would you have responded if you were his parent?
3. Where do you currently have an opportunity to help someone who is going through a rough patch?

CHAPTER 11

1. In your opinion, what are some key characteristics of a good father?
2. What helps you find a positive attitude when life is difficult?
3. What images or memories come to mind when you hear the word *hope*?

CHAPTER 12

1. Who has inspired you in recent weeks?

2. What have you found to be worth fighting for?
3. How will you incorporate prayer into your everyday routines in the coming week?

CHAPTER 13

1. When have you felt deeply blessed through giving to others?
2. How do you typically handle it when people or circumstances try to pull you away from your dreams?
3. Where do you currently need to learn a lesson from a mistake or a "lucky punch"?

CHAPTER 14

1. What's a catchphrase or slogan that describes your philosophy of life?
2. What are some specific ways God has answered your prayers in recent weeks?
3. Where do you have opportunities to connect with good people and/or good causes in your community?

CHAPTER 15

1. Read about Maddux's health setback on pages 106–8. What emotions would you have experienced if you were in Cody's place?
2. What memories or experiences from your own life come to mind when you read those pages?
3. Where do you need a big win right now?

CHAPTER 16

1. How do you typically handle frustration?
2. When you look back at your life, where can you see clear evidence of God's plan and purpose?

3. Read Cody's conversation with Zach on pages 119–20. What is it that you're ultimately fighting for in your life?

CHAPTER 17

1. When have you felt like Cody did walking into that gym: *This is exactly where I'm supposed to be?*
2. How are you currently investing in your dreams?
3. Are you currently more likely to seek out a mentor or to serve as a mentor? What steps can you take this week to move further in that direction?

CHAPTER 18

1. What comes to mind when you think of "the grind"—what does that mean for your life?
2. Do you think it's reasonable to "Stop worrying about the money," as Uriah Faber suggested to Cody? Explain.
3. What gives you confidence, and what can you do to get more?

CHAPTER 19

1. How have you typically handled bullies in your life?
2. Read Cody's conversation with Maddux on pages 149–52. What strikes you as some of the key moments from that connection?
3. Cody has been blessed by Team Alpha Male. How can you maximize the opportunities you have to be part of a community that supports your dreams and challenges you to reach higher?

CHAPTER 20

1. Who are the people in your life who tell you they love you?

2. Cody talks about his prayer life on page 160. How does prayer impact your everyday life and routine?

3. What are some of the factors separating victory and defeat for you right now?

CHAPTER 21

1. Do you believe that life is full of coincidences or that everything is part of a plan? What formed that belief?

2. What are some of the ways Cody demonstrated humility throughout this chapter?

3. Cody mentioned the quote from Marcus Aurelius that "What we do in life echoes in eternity." How have you experienced the truth of that statement?

CHAPTER 22

1. What secrets have you discovered for working through different kinds of pain? How do you keep going?

2. On page 189, Cody talks about the power of staying positive. How have you experienced that power recently?

3. Cody talks a lot about being on "the right path." What helps you know whether you're on that path?

CHAPTER 23

1. What words would you use to describe your experiences with love and romance?

2. On page 188, Cody talks about fist-bumping UFC announcer Bruce Buffer. What would be a similar moment for you and your dreams?

3. How have you experienced the truth that, "When you're on the right path, God provides" (p. 190)?

CHAPTER 24

1. What emotions do you experience when you read the blow-by-blow descriptions of Cody's fights? Why?
2. What challenges have you set your sights on for the next phase of your life?
3. What obstacles will you need to overcome to gain victory in those challenges?

CHAPTER 25

1. What was your favorite part of this chapter? Why?
2. Read about Cody asking for Maddux's picture on pages 204–5. Where do you turn for inspiration and strength when you need them most?
3. Who needs to receive inspiration and strength from you right now?

CHAPTER 26

1. Where will you be, and what will you hear, when you achieve the victory you've been waiting for?
2. What are some of the key themes you have appreciated from this book?
3. What lessons from Cody's story will you apply to your life?

ABOUT THE AUTHORS

CODY GARBRANDT grew up in Uhrichsville, Ohio, where he began boxing at the age of fifteen. With an amateur record of 32–1 in boxing, Cody turned his full attention to the growing sport of Mixed Martial Arts (MMA) after graduating high school. Having compiled a 5–0 record as a professional mixed martial artist, Garbrandt signed with the Ultimate Fighting Championship (UFC) in 2015 and quickly rose through the ranks to become the UFC Bantamweight Champion by defeating Dominick Cruz on December 30, 2016.

Garbrandt is a member of the Team Alpha Male gym in Sacramento, California, where he currently lives with his wife, Danny.

MARK DAGOSTINO is a multiple *New York Times* bestselling coauthor whose career has been built through the sharing of uplifting and inspirational life stories. Before becoming an author, he served ten years on staff in New York and Los Angeles as a well-respected correspondent, columnist, and senior writer for *People* magazine.